Remembering the Parables

Remembering
the Parables

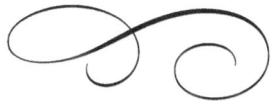

Gary Lee Entsminger
&
Susan Elizabeth Elliott

PINYON PUBLISHING
Montrose, Colorado

Copyright © 2010 by Gary Lee Entsminger & Susan Elizabeth Elliott

All rights reserved. Except as permitted under the U.S. Copyright Act of 1976, no part of this publication may be reproduced, distributed, or transmitted in any form or by any means, or stored in a database or retrieval system, without the prior written permission of the publisher, except for brief quotations in articles, books, and reviews.

Watercolors (pages 49-120 and cover) and back cover photograph copyright © 2010 by Susan E. Elliott

Cover and Book design by Susan E. Elliott

First Edition: 2010

Pinyon Publishing
23847 V66 Trail, Montrose, CO 81403
www.pinyon-publishing.com

Library of Congress Control Number: 2010920550
ISBN: 978-0-9821561-3-1

Special Thanks...

To Dabney Stuart for his helpful comments on an earlier draft of this book.

To Bob Elliott for stimulating conversations about the parables and the early Christian church.

To Joel Kingsolver for insightful cathedral conversations while hiking up Rock Creek in the Colorado Rockies.

for Libby Entsminger
& Elizabeth Rose Elliott

Contents

About this Book   14

JESUS' PARABLES & THE ART OF MEMORY

Jesus' Parables & Sayings
Figurative Language & the Oral Tradition   16
What Did Jesus Say?   20

Learning by Heart: A Child's Memory   22

How to Remember
What is Memory?   26
Intentional Remembering   28
Designing Effective Memory Journeys   30
Creating & Placing Images   36

The Country Church
Parables Journey: The Country Church   42
Parables Images: Seeing & Remembering   50

JESUS' PARABLES

Poems & Paintings
Sower   63
Seed Growing Secretly   65
Wicked Tenants   67
Budding Fig Tree   69

Leaven	71
Treasure	73
Pearl	75
Great Fish	77
Lost Sheep	79
Unforgiving Servant	81
Vineyard Workers	83
Two Sons	85
Lamps & Virgins	87
Talents	89
Wine Bottles	91
Good Samaritan	93
Friend at Midnight	95
Good Gifts	97
Rich Farmer	99
Thief	101
Barren Fig Tree	103
Mustard Seed	105
Great Supper	107
Tower Builder	109
Lost Coin	111
Prodigal Son	113
Unjust Steward	115
Rich Man & Lazarus	117
Unjust Judge	119
Pharisee & Publican	121

Parables in Matthew, Mark, Luke, & Thomas

Sower	122
Seed Growing Secretly	122
Wicked Tenants	123
Budding Fig Tree	124
Leaven	124
Treasure	125
Pearl	125
Great Fish	125
Lost Sheep	126
Unforgiving Servant	126
Vineyard Workers	127
Two Sons	127
Lamps & Virgins	128
Talents	128
Wine Bottles	130
Good Samaritan	131
Friend at Midnight	131
Good Gifts	131
Rich Farmer	132
Thief	132
Barren Fig Tree	133
Mustard Seed	133
Great Supper	133
Tower Builder	135
Lost Coin	135
Prodigal Son	135
Unjust Steward	136

Rich Man & Lazarus	137
Unjust Judge	138
Pharisee & Publican	138

A Deeper Understanding

Remembering Chapters & Verses	140
Mysticism, Meditation, & Sacred Memory	150
Recommended Reading	154
Index	158

To be faithful in a few things.

To be thankful for small favors.

To be undone by the unlikely, the modest.

To be alien in the garden, to look up.

—Dabney Stuart

Mark you the [church] floor? that square and speckled stone,
        Which looks so firm and strong,
            Is Patience:
And th'other black and grave, wherewith each one
        Is checkered all along,
            Humility:
The gentile rising, which on either hand
        Leads to the choir above,
            Is Confidence:
But the sweet cement, which is the one sure band
        Ties the whole frame, is Love
            And Charity.

—George Herbert

About this Book

Some trust in chariots, and some in horses: but we will remember the name of the Lord our God.

—Psalm 20:7

In this book, we present a complete system for remembering the parables of Jesus using the ancient Art of Memory. This easy to learn but powerful memory system can also be used to remember other kinds of information (*e.g.*, lists, tasks, poems, speeches, important dates, and so on).

You may also choose to use this book primarily as a tool to learn more about Jesus' parables and the Art of Memory, without engaging in the Art of Memory yourself. However, we urge you to actively participate in the mnemonic techniques that we walk you through. By practicing the Art of Memory, you will become acquainted with Jesus' parables in a deeper way and grow to see remembering not as a tiresome and time-consuming task but as a relaxing pleasure. See your memories for what they are—treasures and enduring gifts.

This book explores a convergence of two ancient customs: an oral tradition and the Art of Memory. An oral tradition is one that disseminates information by word of mouth. The Art of Memory refers to a specific mental organizational system used to store information. Both of these traditions thrived at the beginning of the Common Era (C.E.; the time period beginning with the year of Christ's birth) when only a small portion of the population of Palestine was literate.

In this book, you will learn the specific Art of Memory techniques that were used in ancient Greece and Rome. As you'll see, the techniques are simple yet extraordinarily powerful if practiced the way ancient orators (*e.g.*, Cicero), Christian figures (*e.g.*, Thomas Aquinas), and modern practitioners (*e.g.*, Dominic O'Brien) have suggested.

Remembering The Parables consists of three parts:

I. Jesus' Parables & The Art of Memory

- Jesus Parables & Sayings
- Learning by Heart: A Child's Memory
- How to Remember
- The Country Church

II. Jesus' Parables

- Poems & Paintings: Thirty of Jesus' parables in poetic form with accompanying art—to help you create your own mnemonic images
- The parables in their King James versions (Matthew, Mark, and Luke) and the Gospel of Thomas—for easy reference

III. A Deeper Understanding

- Remembering Chapters & Verses
- Mysticism, Meditation, & Sacred Memory
- Recommended Reading

A great and beautiful invention is memory,

always useful both for learning and for life.

This is the first thing: if you pay attention

(direct your mind), the judgment will better

perceive the things going through it (the mind).

—the Dialexeis

The Dialexeis *is one of the earliest references to the Art of Memory. Anonymous, it was written in literary Doric sometime just after the Peloponnesian War in ca. 400 B.C.*

Figurative Language & the Oral Tradition

Figurative Language

All this Jesus said to the crowds in parables;

indeed he said nothing to them without a parable.

—Matthew 13:34

You cannot tell people what to do, you can only

tell them parables; and that is what art really is,

particular stories of particular people and experiences.

—W. H. Auden

Jesus taught in figurative language. He compared the kingdom of heaven to leaven, to treasure, to merchants. He indicated how people should live in the kingdom by telling vivid and sometimes puzzling parables. Some of these parables suggest reversals of expectations. Humble men inherit the earth. A Samaritan unexpectedly does good deeds. A prodigal son disappoints his father then repents and returns home. Very small things, like mustard seeds, grow into majestic and great products. Some of Jesus' teachings appear simple. A man sells everything to buy a field or a pearl. Someone draws in a net full of mostly small fishes, and he throws back all except one great one. Other parables are longer, more complex stories with twists and turns of plot. For example, the Good Samaritan, the Vineyard Workers, and the Unjust Steward. All of the parables contain tangible and vivid images. These images make the parables memorable.

Understanding the Parables

Christians, religious scholars, and even non-Christians have debated what these mysterious parables mean for two thousand years. In our Recommended Reading section near the end of this book, we've listed some of these parable interpreters (*e.g.*, Perrin, Crossan, and Jeremias). We encourage you to explore some of their excellent and thoughtful books. However, we won't try to explain what the parables mean here. Instead, this book helps you remember what they are, and especially—the images that compose the parables. If you remember a parable, you carry it with you, in your memory and in your heart. As the great writer, Franz Kafka wrote, "If you only followed the parables you yourselves would become parables." Carrying an item with you consciously or unconsciously and thinking about what you carry leads to greater understanding. As we all know, some of our deepest feelings cannot be expressed in words. When our actions begin to illustrate those inexpressible ideals, we start to live the parables; we start to live Jesus' teachings.

Oral Tradition & the Art of Memory

Many of us first learned about the parables of Jesus through a form of oral tradition. We listened while our parents, Sunday School teachers, and preachers told us the stories of Jesus. Similarly, most Bible scholars believe that the sayings of Jesus originally circulated through Palestine via an oral tradition. Since writing did not become widespread until the eighth century, in Jesus' day, oral traditions probably included some type of mnemonic (memory) method. During this same time period, Greek and Roman orators (*e.g.*, Cicero) used the Art of Memory to remember speeches. Numerous Latin documents detail the use of the Art of Memory since ancient times. Because the Art of Memory had been used at least 500 years earlier in nearby Greece, and since Greek was the primary language of the New Testament in the first few centuries C.E., some of Jesus' followers might have used the Art of Memory to remember and share Jesus' teachings.

Persons desiring to train memory must select places, form mental images of the things they wish to remember, and store those images in the places, so that the order of the places will preserve the order of the things, and the images of the things will denote the things themselves, and we shall employ the places and images respectively as a wax writing tablet and the letters written on it.

—Cicero

Marcus Tullius Cicero (106 B.C.-43 B.C.) was a Roman philosopher who wrote widely on oratory. His work on the Art of Memory is some of the earliest now known.

The Art of Memory was well-known during ancient times and the Middle Ages, and it peaked during the Renaissance (Yates 1966). Most references to the Art of Memory appear only when writing became more common. During these later centuries, the Art of Memory was adopted as a powerful spiritual technique by many prominent Christian figures, (*e.g.*, Thomas Aquinas, Giordano Bruno, and St. Ignatius Loyola). Loyola's "The Spiritual Exercises" (composed from 1522-1524) consists of a set of meditations, prayers, and mental exercises that use the Art of Memory for remembering events in Jesus' life.

Early Collections of Jesus Teachings

We don't have the earliest written documents describing Jesus' teachings. We only have copies. Scholars hypothesize that the earliest documents were organized in such a way to suggest translation from an oral tradition. For example, these early documents probably consisted of sayings and lacked the narrative structure found in later documents.

A "missing" first century collection of Jesus' sayings that preceded the synoptic gospels (*i.e.*, Matthew, Mark, and Luke) has been hypothesized by biblical scholars since the beginning of the 19th century (*e.g.*, by Herbert Marsh, a bishop in the Church of England). These sayings were perhaps circulating as early as the apostle Paul's epistles (*ca.* 50-60 C.E.). One of these "sayings gospels" has been named "Q," or the "Q Gospel," for the German "Quelle," meaning "source." A minimalist (or conservative) version of "Q" consists of sayings that are found both in Matthew and Luke but not in Mark.

Some scholars (*e.g.*, Stephen J. Patterson and John D. Crossan) have hypothesized a "Common Sayings gospel" based on sayings found in both Q and the Gnostic Gospel of Thomas. Both of these sayings gospels (Q and the Gospel of Thomas) lack the narrative structure of the New Testament gospels. Thus, they might represent an oral tradition that preceded the New Testament. Oral traditions, such as one aided by the Art of Memory, preserve information as lists or organized groups of concise pieces of data, events, or details, without narrative details. At this time, we lack sufficient information about the first century to prove much about who, when, or how Jesus' sayings and parables were actually preserved. But we know from current experience that we can use the Art of Memory to remember these sayings and parables—that is, to know Jesus teachings by heart.

I will open my mouth in Parables, I will utter things that have been kept secret from the foundation of the world.

Things strange yet common, incredible, yet known; most high, yet plain; infinitely profitable, but not esteemed.

Is it not a great thing that you should be Heir of the World?

—*Thomas Traherne*

What Did Jesus Say?

A parable is a figure of speech in which a comparison is made between God's kingdom, actions, or expectations and something in this world, real or imagined.

—Arland J. Hultgren

In This Book
We focus on 30 parables that:

• *almost everyone agrees are indeed "parables"*

• *are arguably Jesus' most prominent and reliable parables*

• *occur in Matthew, Mark, and/or Luke (the synoptic gospels)*

• *may also occur in the Gnostic Gospel of Thomas*

• *often occur in more than one gospel*

How Many Parables?

It depends on whom you ask and how you define "parable." Here, we define a parable as a saying of Jesus (*i.e.*, information he is reputed to have said) which includes story-like actions and concrete images versus a simpler saying, or "aphorism," that gives you more abstract advice on how to live.

Scholars and clergymen, each with their own variation on how to define a parable, generally classify between 30 and 60 of Jesus' sayings as parables. The "New Schofield Reference Bible," 1967 edition of the King James version called 37 of Jesus' sayings, "parables." All of these 37 parables occur in the synoptic gospels: Matthew, Mark, and Luke. The Jesus Seminar ("The Parables of Jesus, Red Letter Edition") critically evaluated 33 of Jesus' parables. John Dominic Crossan in his classic study, "In Parables, The Challenge of the Historic Jesus," examined 37 parables, but settled on a smaller number as being reliable parables. Kyle R. Snodgrass, in "Stories with Intent," studied 30 parables in depth. And so on. One gets a slightly different number and a slightly different set of parables with each scholar.

Choosing Parables to Remember

After examining numerous bibles (old and revised, from various denominations and centuries), we chose the 37 parables included in the "New Schofield Reference Bible" as a starting point. Reverend Schofield wrote his commentaries (which indicate whether a passage is a parable) in the 1910s and 1920s. Although Schofield usually used the cue "parable" in the text to demarcate a parable, he didn't always. Some parables that aren't specifically called "parables" seem like parables. But some parables that are called "parables" seem more like aphorisms than parables. Thus, the scholars and modern theologians have ample room for debate. We listened to many of their arguments and decided on 30 parables that were generally accepted by liberal and conservative scholars alike. We discuss another 60 or so sayings that seem to us to represent the core of Jesus' teachings elsewhere.

Parable Order Sequence

Since we can't tell from Matthew, Mark, and Luke the order Jesus told the parables in (because the order varies among sources), and it seems most likely that he told and retold the parables many times, we don't think a particular order is important for remembering them. However, some order IS important for remembering!

Since most modern biblical scholars consider Mark to be an older text than Matthew or Luke, we've generally listed the parables that occur in Mark first, then Matthew, then Luke. We list the parable chapter and verse references, including the text for each parable on pages 122-138. At a glance, you can see how many times, and where, a parable appears in the New Testament.

These are the hidden words which he who lives spoke and he, Judas Didymos Thomas, wrote down. And He said this: "Whoever finds the meaning of these words, he shall not taste Death."

—The Gospel of Thomas

Compare your Sources:

Sometimes parables in different gospels are very similar and sometimes not. We think you might enjoy comparing them yourself, so on pages 122-138, we show you the 30 parables side by side in their King James versions (Matthew, Mark, and Luke) and in the Gospel of Thomas where appropriate.

Learning by Heart: A Child's Memory

> *When I remember these things, I pour out my soul in me: for I had gone with the multitude, I went with them to the house of God, with the voice of joy and praise, with a multitude that kept holyday.*
>
> —Psalm 42:4

When we were Young

We grew up in different parts of the country, during different decades, yet we learned to remember in similar ways: through games, songs, and fun activities with friends and families.

In a rural California town in the 1980s, in one church at the start of Sunday school, all the children met in one large room for music. An easel in the front held a jumbo pad of paper with a song on each page. To accompany the lyrics, the song leaders drew colorful symbols to represent the words (*e.g.*, a heart for Love, a dove for Peace). In this way, children learned the songs before they could read the words. And even for those who could read, the images were cues—they sparked memories as they sang.

In rural Virginia, in the 1950s, young children were encouraged to memorize psalms and other biblical verses in Bible and Sunday school. They stood on the church steps on a warm humid morning in July and took turns reciting psalms to their friends sitting on the grass. It was a game, and learning was fun. Enthusiastically, children sang the songs and repeated the psalms, time and again.

And our memories of many of those songs and psalms are as strong today as they were when we were five or six years old.

For many of us, the game continued. The more songs we learned, the easier it was to learn new ones. We memorized hundreds of popular songs, as well as nursery rhymes, stories, newspaper headlines, names and makes of cars, baseball statistics, our dozens of cousins, ballet and Tai Chi exercises, and anything else we wanted to remember. It came naturally. It was a game.

Learning by Heart

We called our remembering "learning by heart." But only recently have we thought to ask: Why was it called learning by heart? Was learning by heart any different from what we now know as "memorizing?" And how did we do it?

The ancient Greeks believed that the heart, the most noticeable internal organ, was the seat of intelligence, memory, and emotion. Our word, "record," derives from the Middle English word for "to recall," and from the Latin, *recordari*, meaning "from the heart" (Robert Hendrickson, Encyclopedia of Word and Phrase Origins, 1997).

Relating learning by heart and scripture, Ebenezer Cobham Brewer in The Dictionary of Phrase and Fable (1905) wrote:

> *The heart is the seat of understanding; thus the Scripture speaks of men wise in heart and slow of heart. To learn by rote is to learn so as to be able to repeat. To learn by memory is to commit to memory without reference to understanding what is so learnt. To learn by heart is to learn and understand.*

Today, more than one hundred years after Brewer published his definition, the concept of learning by heart has been collapsed in a modern interpretation. "By heart" is now simply defined as "to learn by rote," which in turn means "to learn by repetition, often without full attention or comprehension" (The American Heritage Dictionary, Fourth Edition, 2000).

Man cannot understand without images; the image is a similitude of a corporeal thing, but understanding is of universals which are to be abstracted from particulars.

—Thomas Aquinas

Thomas Aquinas (1225-1274) was an Italian priest of the Roman Catholic Church. He wrote about the Art of Memory and was renowned for his outstanding memory.

> *Wherefore one best learns by studying from illuminated books, for the different colors bestow remembrance of the different lines and consequently of that thing which one wants to get by heart.*
>
> —from a Fifteenth Century French *ars memorativa,* translated by Mary Carruthers

Were we children learning all those songs by pure rote—without giving the task our full attention? We don't think so. Repetition is an essential ingredient in any memory practice, but it is not the sole ingredient. We suspect that these "repetition" oriented definitions indicate a shift in how people often think about memory and remembering, a shift that might also explain why we forget so much.

Instead of being the seat of intelligence, memory, and emotion, the heart has now become known as "a hollow muscular organ of vertebrate animals that by its rhythmic contraction acts as a force pump maintaining the circulation of the blood" (Merriam-Webster's Collegiate Dictionary, Eleventh Edition, 2008). The seat of intelligence has been usurped by the brain, which controls autonomic function such as heartbeat. However, memorization by automaton brain function without calling on the creative imaginative heart and soul is unlikely to be long-lasting. Most of our daily bombardment by information goes in one ear (or eye) and out the other. Has classifying our heart and brain as pump and control center made us feel like passive involuntary machines? Pump and control center may be the biological functions of heart and mind, but then how do we talk about, use, and understand our soul and spirit, our inspiration, imagination, and instinct? By focusing solely on the biological functions of heart and mind, have we been closing the curtain on the active imaginative learning style that Jesus demonstrated with his parables?

Heart-Mind Learning

Recently we've observed a gradual reemergence of a more holistic idea of heart-mind learning (Childre and Martin, The HeartMath Solution, 2000). Heart-mind learning combines the emotional and imaginative with the analytical and structured to achieve the goal of fully internalizing, understanding, and remembering. This time-tested tradition of structuring our imagination was fundamental to our childhood learning process, but it is often abandoned as we grow older and become less playful.

The Art of Memory provides structure for remembering the symbolic images we create. We simply associate images with the things we want to remember. Then we place those images in locations so we can go back and find them again. The parables of Jesus are at their simplest—metaphors or symbolic images arranged as stories. These images come almost ready-made for remembering. The work of remembering consists primarily of attention, a desire to remember, and a willingness to order one's memory. By practicing the simple memory techniques described here, we can brighten our emotional and physical lives.

It is impossible even to think without a mental picture.

—Aristotle

What is Memory?

There are then two kinds of memory: one natural and the other the product of art. The natural memory is that memory which is imbedded in our minds, born simultaneously with thought. The artificial memory is that memory which is strengthened by a kind of training and system of discipline.

—Ad Herennium

The *Rhetorica Ad Herennium was written in the first century B.C. It was long attributed to Cicero but is now considered to be the work of one of his contemporaries. It is the earliest known book that discusses the Art of Memory in detail.*

The terms short-term and long-term memory are familiar to most of us. Short-term memory (also called primary, active, or working memory) refers to our capacity for holding information in the mind in a readily available state for a short period of time. Studies suggest that without rehearsal or active maintenance, the duration of short-term memory is a few seconds. Estimates of short-term memory capacity vary among individuals and depend on the experimental design used to estimate capacity. Typically, one can hold a list of four to nine elements in his or her short-term memory (on average, 7 ± 2 elements, Kenneth L. Higbee, "Your Memory: How It Works and How to Improve It"). In contrast, we can store a potentially unlimited amount of information indefinitely in long-term memory.

We can also contrast short- and long-term memories as automatic and robotic versus willful and intentional. Most of what passes through our short-term awareness is forgotten because we don't try to remember it. To remember something for a long period of time, we usually have to want to remember it. Exceptions might be tragic or pleasurable events that stand out, which we often remember without trying.

In this book, we show you how to improve your long-term intentional memory. We use a memory system that has been practiced for at least 2500 years. Through the centuries, this technique has been called the Art of Memory (*ars memoria*), sacred memory (*sacra memoria*), *spiritalis memoria, sancta memoria, ars notoria*, the monastic Art of Memory, and the meditative way. Ancient Greeks and Romans (*e.g.*, Cicero), theologians and monks of the Middle Ages (*e.g.*, Thomas Aquinas), philosophers and scholars of the Renaissance (*e.g.*, Giordano Bruno), and modern memory masters (*e.g.*, Dominic O'Brien) have used this system. One compilation of methods, "The New Art of Memory," by M. Gregor Von Feinaigle in 1813, describes at least seventy-five well-known variations of the *ars memoria*. In the following sections, we will walk you through the basic steps in this widely-used ancient memory art.

> *There are four things which help a man to remember well.*
>
> *The first is that he should dispose those things which he wishes to remember in a certain order.*
>
> *The second is that he should adhere to them with affection.*
>
> *The third is that he should reduce them to unusual similitudes.*
>
> *The fourth is that he should repeat them with frequent meditation.*
>
> —the Dialexeis

Intentional Remembering

> *Only people with a powerful memory know what they are going to say and for how long they are going to speak and in what style, what points they have already answered and what still remains.*
>
> —Cicero

Intentional remembering using the Art of Memory has two basic components: images and places. To remember one item, you picture an image or symbol that represents that item, and you put it in a dedicated place. That is, you associate the image with what you want to remember, and you associate the image with its place. Our minds naturally associate images. The trick here is to intentionally associate images and places.

To remember a list of items, you create a series of places (or locations), one for each item you want to remember. We call the series of places a memory journey. You imagine this journey, and you step through the journey, associating images with places. When you want to recall an item, you return to the journey and go to the place where you put its image. There, you *remember* the image and in turn, the item, event, or other information the image represents.

With a little practice, you will be able to move immediately to a place in your journey and retrieve the desired information. You'll also be able to list the images or items in order, backwards or forwards. As you practice remembering with memory journeys, you'll surprise yourself by how easily and how much you can remember at will.

Thomas Aquinas said in his "*Summa Theologica*" that you should be interested in what you want to remember. In other words, we must want to remember for the Art of Memory to work. Aquinas also said that "we better recall things that we understand through contemplation." Similarly, the modern memory master, Dominic

O'Brien, suggests reviewing what you've remembered just after you've done the memorization and reviewing again at lengthening intervals to keep the information fresh and available.

In summary, to remember using the Art of Memory:
1. Create a memory journey of places/locations.
2. Form vivid mental images that represent the items you want to remember. Place those images along the journey, one key image for each place.
3. Review your journey with a heart of desire.

Next, we'll describe the first two steps of the Art of Memory at length. For more on remembering with a heart of desire and memory meditations, see Mysticism, Meditation, and Sacred Memory (page 152).

The first of these things is that he should find certain mental images that match the things he wants to remember. But this should not be at all usual: because we marvel more at things which are unusual, and the soul is held by such things more and with greater force: whence it happens that we remember more those things that we see in childhood.

—Thomas Aquinas

Designing Effective Memory Journeys

Prepare Journeys in Advance

It's both efficient and rewarding to prepare memory journeys in advance. The more journeys you create, the more places you'll have ready for new memories. When you want to remember a new list of items, you'll already have a place to put them. If your wife calls with seven items to add to the grocery list, you can quickly place them (by seeing each item) in a ready-made memory journey, without needing to scramble for pen and paper or having to make up a journey on the spot. Image a journey you've taken, a place where you've lived, your dream house, or even your next vacation. It's simply picturing places you already know or would like to know. Then you divide each place, or setting, into a distinct number of locations. It's play, and once you have a journey, you've done most of the work. You can create journeys anytime: while driving to work (but be careful not to drive to your memory journey location), washing dishes, walking/exercising, or waiting for an appointment. Also, creating journeys is excellent practice for remembering new things later. You exercise and improve your memory by creating and meditating on your journeys. Once you've created a journey, you'll discover memories along the way. And you'll want to return to them!

For remembering Jesus' parables, we've created a journey for you that takes place in and around a hypothetical country church. We'll describe this country church at length on pages 52-59.

[If he wanted to remember a discourse] he would take a house, for instance, either the one in which he might deliver the discourse, or another; with every part which he was perfectly acquainted. He would begin at some fixed point of that house, suppose the right side of the door, and he would proceed round it in circular fashion... He would transfer each of the symbols to the different compartments of the house.

—M. Gregor Von Feinaigle

M. Gregor Von Feinaigle (1760-1819) was a German mnemonist and educator. His book, "The New Art of Memory," is a compilation of memory techniques and variations.

Make Familiar Journeys

Until you've had some practice, we suggest you make your first journeys ones you're familiar with. A journey can be around your house, your yard, through a nearby woods, through a school grounds, or from city to city. Journeys can be short or long, inside or outside, true journeys that you remember or journeys you make up. They can be journeys from your past or journeys you're planning to make (trip itineraries). You might use your beds of roses, irises, sunflowers, marigolds, and columbines to indicate a journey of five places. Or your living room, kitchen, family room, bathroom, and bedroom would make another journey of five. Anything can work, as long as you can see each stop (place or location) clearly in your mind.

Most journeys will be specific and original to each of us. For example, the order of rooms in our childhood homes will vary. Maybe you had two bathrooms, while we had one. Maybe you had a basement, and we had none. Perhaps you had an attic you played in. The more personal and familiar the journey is to you, the better it will stick with you, like taffy. Or perhaps you prefer cotton candy.

Order Journey Places/Locations

Order the locations along your journey (1, 2,...n), so that each time you move through your journey, you see the places in the same order. The natural "walking order" of your journey works best. That is, order the locations in the same sequence you would reach them in if you were walking naturally from one place to the

Settings for Memory Journeys

- *Rooms or walls in your house*
- *School grounds*
- *Work place*
- *Church or community center*
- *Gym*
- *Shopping center*
- *Fast food restaurant*
- *Playground*
- *Driving route (to work, school, groceries, mall, a friend's house)*
- *Walking route through a neighborhood*
- *Familiar hike at the beach or mountains*
- *Trip itinerary*
- *Body parts*
- *Parts of other items (animals, cars, musical instruments, tools)*
- *First 10 things you do in the morning*
- *Homes of each of your family members*

next. For example, an easy journey to remember could consist of the five places you see or go to first each morning. Make the order logical for you. For one of us, we start in our

1. Bedroom

Then we visit the

2. Bathroom

Then we stumble down the

3. Stairs

Thankfully, next, we arrive by the coffee pot in the

4. Kitchen

And, now, ready to greet the day, we pick up the newspaper that is waiting for us on the

5. Front Step

> *Everyone carries a room about inside him. This can be proved by the sense of hearing. If someone walks fast and listens, say in the night, when everything round about is quiet, one hears, for instance, the rattling of a mirror not quite firmly fastened to the wall.*
>
> —Franz Kafka

Break Down a Long Journey into Smaller Journeys

Start with short journeys of five or ten locations. Then build up to longer journeys. At first, don't try to remember anything besides the journey. For practice, mentally walk through your journey. Look around, observe, and remember.

Each time you remember five new places, it's simply a repeat of the exercise to remember five more places. Places sixty-one to sixty-five are just as easy to remember as places one to five. You'll find that with a little practice, ten will become an easy, efficient number of items or places to work with at a time. As soon as you remember the first ten, you can remember the second ten just as easily.

Designate Landmark Locations

If your complete journey has more than five or ten locations, mark each fifth or tenth place to remind you where you are in your numbering. If you need to jump to item 13, you simply go three locations past the tenth location (versus counting up all the way from one). Often the exact order of the images you're remembering doesn't matter, but sometimes it does, say, The Periodic Table of Elements. Order helps remembering go smoothly. If you reach your special location number five, but you know you've only listed three items so far, you know you've skipped a location. So you can stop and retrace your steps before you get too far along your journey.

For example, you could make up a funny idea about a landmark location, or you could place something significant there. If it's a basketball court at the tenth location, maybe it's an extra special court where everyone is lifting you to their shoulders and cheering for you, the winner. If it's a sand box, have a huge shovel with a "1" written on it and a huge bucket with a "0." If it's a dining room, think "Great! We can chow down. This is a super spot!" If you think about these landmark locations a hair longer than the other locations, it will help you to remember that they're special.

Picture Your Journey

Close your eyes and picture each place along your route. What stands out? When you come to a gate, is it white or some other color? Wood or metal? Open or closed? Details make places memorable. The longer you spend on this step, the more fun you'll have, and the easier it will be to remember the actual images you place there later.

Memorize the Journey

Learn each location in your journey by heart so you can easily move from one location to the next. Some people like to feel themselves hovering or flying from one location to the next. Others prefer to walk upright from one place to the next. Get some mental exercise; locomote through your journey until you're confident you won't pass up a location. If you have a "trouble" location (one you skip over or come to out of order), adjust your journey or give the location some special attention. Remembering is mostly a matter of ordering the places, seeing your journey clearly, and wanting to remember.

Match Journeys to What You're Remembering

As you become adept at creating journeys, you'll find it useful to use journeys that are appropriate to what you want to remember. If you're remembering information about William Shakespeare's plays, you might want to create a journey in a playhouse, where the location itself is a trigger for remembering. If you're remembering a chemical formula or the Periodic Table of Elements, you might want to walk around your Chemistry lab. Recipes work well in a kitchen. Speeches are appropriate in the auditorium or seminar room where you'll give the speech.

> *What we need to know is how the imagination thinks. Or, to turn it another way, how the human being thinks with his imagination; how he thinks in pictures.*
>
> —Elizabeth Sewell

What You Gain from Memory Journeys

Remember—the journeys themselves have additional power because they remind you of your life, of places you've been, of places you imagined you wanted to go. For example, when you create a journey in a place from your past (*e.g.*, your childhood home, elementary school, or park you played in), each time you return to this journey, you will likely discover "new" memories from the place you hadn't thought of in a long time. When walking through your high school again, you might suddenly see a classmate you haven't consciously thought about in years. You will occasionally even see people or items you didn't consciously notice long ago. Your memory is a marvel of information and mysteries.

Creating & Placing Images

Create Images to Represent what you want to Remember

To make the most of the Art of Memory: observe, describe, and imagine. You use these natural skills to create images to associate with the things or ideas you want to remember. If you're remembering ten lines of poetry, you might have ten images, each representing a line of the poem. When you remember the 30 parables, you'll begin by creating an image to associate with each parable. Then you'll place these images at each of the 30 locations on your journey. Your goal is to create one clear key image that represents each item you're trying to remember.

Associate Images

If you're trying to remember an item, word, or concept, you create an association between it and an image. For Love, you might imagine a heart; for Peace, a dove. For God's Promise, you might imagine a wedding ring or a rainbow. In addition to traditional symbols like these, associations can be spelling-based. For example, to remember the disciple Matthew, you might imagine a mat or a math symbol: the symbol for pi or even your math teacher. If you have a friend named Matthew, you might picture him before anything else, so the image of your friend, Matthew, can represent the disciple Matthew.

Say you're remembering the Ten Commandments, and you want

Whenever you hear something, connect it with what you know already.

—the Dialexeis

Association

"something linked in memory or imagination with a thing or person" or *"the process of forming mental connections or bonds between sensations, ideas, or memories."*

—Merriam-Webster's Collegiate Dictionary, Eleventh Edition

to remember "You shall not have any other gods before me." What's the first thing you think of?... gods before me... Perhaps you see a queue, a line of people waiting for something, other people before others. Are they patient or anxious? What are they waiting for? Just think about the image for a moment... What about "You shall not steal."? Maybe you see a shoplifter or a mugger running down the street with police chasing from behind. Do you hear someone call "Stop! Thief!" Or do you hear police whistles? Can you feel the wind on the face of the thief running? Add these tangible details to personalize your images.

This might sound difficult, but it's already something we do naturally, whether consciously or unconsciously. If someone mentions a mutual friend, an image of that friend or another image you associate with that friend will usually leap into your mind. You might see that friend's home or an event you associate with her. If someone mentions a movie star or famous athlete, say Mickey Mantle, you might see an image of Yankee stadium or a baseball cap. The specifics of the image you see matter only to you.

Don't work too hard to find the "perfect" image to associate with what you want to remember. The image that comes into your mind first, without effort, is often the best. Remember—your memory is working for, not against, you. Our memories love to associate, so it comes naturally. Relax, close your eyes if you need to, and something will appear.

Association Practice

On your own or with a friend, say words (take turns) or randomly point at words in a book or newspaper, and quickly say the first thing you think of when you hear or see that word.

For example, we played this game with ourselves and had the following responses. When one said "fisherman," the other saw "net." When one said "ant," the other saw "an ant hill." Wealth? - a stack of bills. Family? - a mom. Hardship? - people limping.

The associations may seem bizarre sometimes, but that can be all the better. Mostly you'll find how natural and fun this process is.

Describe Images

The more striking the image, the more likely you are to remember it. Exaggerate; make the image look silly, scary, or comforting—whatever works for you.

The images you create must be memorable but needn't be elaborate or even greatly detailed. Sometimes simple images that aren't cluttered with surplus details are the most memorable. To remember a saint, for example Saint Francis of Assisi, the patron saint of animals and the environment, you might picture a bird. For Saint Michael, the patron saint of chivalry, you might picture a sword or a dragon. For Mary Magdalene, an ointment jar. The key is that you see the image in your mind and associate that image with what you want to remember.

If you have trouble conjuring the image clearly in your mind, ask yourself how your five senses respond to the image. Sometimes exaggerated images are more memorable. When you remember the Great Fish parable, make the fish huge—even a whale, splashing all over the church. How does the image make you feel emotionally (scared, amused)? What colors are included in the image? Can you hear anything associated with the image (the sizzle of something frying on the stove, church bells, sleigh bells, traffic, pounding, wind howling, laughter)? How does the image feel to the touch (soft, rough, wet, heavy)? Does the image have a smell (like fresh bread, a fish market, new snow, roses, peppermint)? Can you taste the image? Imagine licking it.

The image thus gives quality, creates atmosphere, and conveys emotion in a way no precise description, however clear and accurate, can possibly do.

—Caroline Spurgeon

All you need to do is form a mental picture of each [symbol] and see them at the stops along the route. You can use a number of tools to aid your imagination, such as exaggeration, color, humor, and movement... also, use all five senses of sight, sound, smell, taste, and touch.

—Dominic O'Brien

Practice Image making

Try this simple exercise to develop your mental imaging skill. Select an object that is near you, say a teapot. While looking at the teapot closely describe it aloud or to yourself. Then close your eyes and picture the teapot. Note as many details as you can. Then open your eyes and look at the teapot again. Note what you missed the first time and try again. Repeat the process several times or until you see the teapot clearly in your mind.

Use all of your senses. How large is the teapot? Is it hot to the touch? Is it heavy? Can you smell what type of tea is being brewed? Can you hear anything as someone pours tea into a cup? How does the tea taste when you sip it?

Note that images are symbolic. For example, you could use a teapot image to remember the city of Boston (making the Boston Tea Party association). Make the teapot as large as you want. Maybe it's gigantic and bobbing about in the ocean, slopping bits of brown tea into the waves. Images that are funny or unusual are often the most memorable. Make the image something you enjoy seeing and you'll enjoy remembering it.

We can also recall an object by one of its attributes; in this manner, we recall sweetness from a depiction of a tub of honey, ferocity from a lion, and wrath from a bear.

—Giordano Bruno

Seeing Images
Note that looking closely at the objects before you and describing them (to yourself, aloud, in a notebook) will improve your ability to see and make mental images. Begin to see more detail whenever you look at anything.

Secure Images to Journey Locations

After you've created an image for something you want to remember, place that image at a particular location on your journey. Perhaps the first stage of a story you're remembering involves the city of Boston. If you're using a journey of the first things you do in the morning, the first location might be your bed. Therefore, see that big warm teapot on your bed.

He who enters through the gate of hearing is armed with his voice and with speech, the son of voice.

He who enters through the gate of vision is armed with suitable forms, gestures, motions and figures.

He who enters through the gate of the imagination, mind and reason is armed with customs and the arts.

—Giordano Bruno

Giordano Bruno (1548-1600) was born in Nola, Italy. He was a philosopher and mathematician. His scientific views were well-advanced of his times. For example, he was a proponent of the heliocentric view of the cosmos. He wrote extensively about the Art of Memory. He was burned at the stake by the Roman Inquisition.

To secure your image to the location (so that whenever you return to your bed in your mind, you see the teapot, for example), think about why the image is there and how you feel about its being there. For example, you could make up a reason for the teapot being on your bed: "Oh yes," you say, "I love having tea brought to me in bed." Of course this story doesn't have to be true, but it's fun, and you might enjoy remembering it. Alternatively, perhaps you see that very large teapot spilling tea all over your bed. "Goodness," you say. "This teapot is making a mess. Or is my bed a water bed?" This is a funny scene, one that may be more memorable than a small nondescript teapot sitting on a corner of your bed, blending in with the bedspread.

As you review your memory journeys you may find yourself asking: "Now what is on the bed? Why?" And because you've created a logical, albeit pretend, story about the image at that location, you'll be able to respond: "Oh yes, of course, I have tea in bed," or "Oh yes, that darn teapot is wetting my sheets." Perhaps the teapot is "wetting the bed." Slightly vulgar, but memorable! And without anxiety, you easily know that your story starts with the image of a teapot. So of course, it reminds you of what that teapot is associated with: Boston.

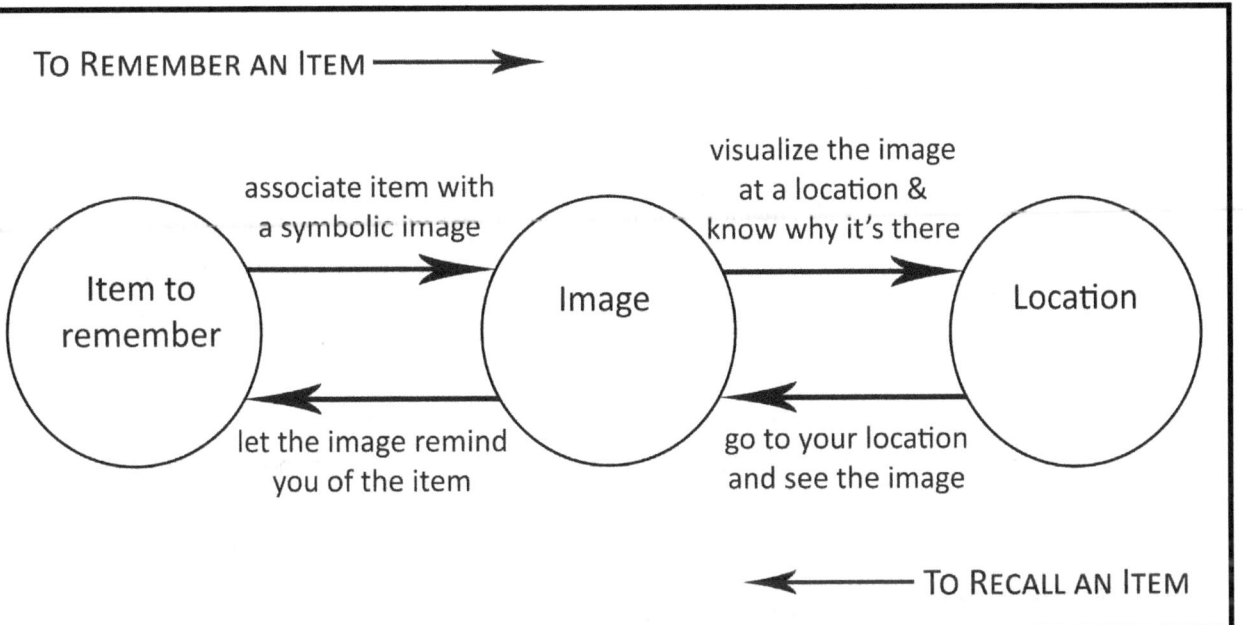

Own Your Images

As you practice, you'll find your mind handling the work of making clear associations and binding them to the location with your logical stories. This will become second nature; you'll do it without realizing it. But in the beginning, the more attention you pay to making your images, the quicker your learning will go.

By the end of this book, you'll have many images located throughout a simple country church. To make each image memorable, you should make up a story for why it's there. Each image will be personalized (by you) so it will stick with you. Each image will remind you of a parable and connect you personally to that parable.

Parables Journey: The Country Church

The artificial memory includes backgrounds and images. By backgrounds I mean such scenes as are naturally or artificially set off on a small scale, complete and conspicuous, so that we can grasp and embrace them easily by the natural memory—for example, a house, an inter-columnar space, a recess, an arch, or the like.

An image is, as it were, a figure, mark, or portrait of the object we wish to remember; for example, if we wish to recall a horse, a lion, or an eagle, we must place its image in a definite background.

—Ad Herennium

A memory journey should always contain places that make logical sense to you. Since the parables have a strong association for many of us with a church or other place of worship, we think it's logical to use a journey through a church for remembering the parables. Since we all have some image of a church in our minds, we strongly suggest you picture your own church or another church that has strong memories for you. For example, you might remember the church you attended as a child.

Here, we describe a simple country church. First we'll walk you through the church so you can see it in your mind. We want you to see this church clearly, but it need only be an example for your imagination, a template. Regardless of which church you see, make it a church you would enjoy returning to when you need to recall something. It can be anywhere and look the way you want it to. It doesn't even need to be a church. It could be a school room, for example. Just adapt the types of details we use to whatever you see in your mind. Our country church is non-denominational and contains generic features found in most, if not all churches (steps, pews, windows, altar, pulpit, steeple, and so on).

After describing this church where our memory journey takes place, we'll pinpoint the 30 locations that you can use for remembering the 30 parables. But for now, we invite you to share the whole image with us.

The Country Church

Imagine a small church on the side of a steep mountain in the southern Appalachians. Although built from rough-cut boards made from the surrounding deciduous woods, the church has recently been painted white. See the white paint. See the boards fitting together not quite perfectly. Feel the narrowness of this warm country building. See the woods around the church. Which season is it? Is it winter with a dusting of snow? Spring with vagrant daffodils popping up beside the church steps? Summer with sweat dripping down your face? Fall with leaves crunching and in a kaleidoscope around you? Look, be there.

At the front of the church, steps lead up to a small porch, its roof supported by two stout posts. The porch looks small but sturdy. The posts are strong sentinels. Add your own details. How many people could stand on the porch at a time? Do the boards creek when you stand on them? From the porch a door leads into the church. How large is the door? Which way does it open? Is it painted? Is there a sign on it? Is the sun hitting it? Or is it in shadow?

When you open the door and step inside you are in what we refer to as the back of the church. You notice immediately how simple the designers have been and how small the expected congregation was. Three wooden pews sit on each side of a center aisle. Start walking down the nave, the center of the church. The nave floors are smooth, brown boards. You can still smell the pine that made them.

In the center of the church, with the center pews at your left and right, look to your left. You see two tall windows. One just between the back and center pews and another between the center and front pews. Now look to your right, the same pattern: pew, window, pew, window, pew.

Now walk up to the center front of the church. A thick oak altar has a bible lying open on it. On the left side of the altar a well-crafted pulpit stands waiting for the preacher. Behind the pulpit in the corner is a choir loft. At the far wall, behind the altar, is a simple baptismal font. And in the right corner of the building, next to the font, an old upright piano has seen better days but still sounds great!

Now that you've seen the inside of the church, walk outside again: down the center of the church, through the door, to the porch, down the steps. Take a few steps away from the church so you can see it well. Look up. Can you see the steeple? What does the roof look like? Are the shingles old or new?

Turn your gaze to the left side of the church; it's a small lawn or patch of grassy weeds. You wonder if kids play there. You see that just in front of the church, to the left of the steps, a sign marks the church name or a Sunday sermon topic. And where are you standing? The parking area. It's mostly dirt, but you can see how the cars can cram in here on Sunday morning. Now look to the right of the church. There's a small building back toward the woods. It's the parsonage.

Over to the right of the buildings toward the trees you notice some gravestones. There is a small wooden fence surrounding this church cemetery. Walk through the open gate. The first grave maker is a rounded marble stone, lichened with age. Next to this sturdy gravestone is a simple wooden cross marking the grave of a child's death. Shading these graves is an old spreading oak.

This is our country church. Review it in your mind. How many pews were inside? How many windows? Notice intricacies. In the front left and right corners—music—the choir and the piano. When just inside the church, the steeple would be right above you. When you feel comfortable with the church and churchyard, move onto the next section, where we outline the specific locations where you will place images representing the parables.

Journey Locations 1-30

We split the country church memory journey into groups of five. Memorize the first five locations. Then add another five and review all ten. Then memorize five more and review the 15, and so on.

Recall that as a rule, we refer to the side of the church you walk in (with the door, porch, and steeple) as the back of the church. The front of the church is where you find the altar, pulpit, choir, font, and piano.

1-5

Let's say it's a warm spring or fall day, and you begin your journey at the steps of the church. The beginning of this memory journey consists of the following five locations:

1. Steps
2. Porch
3. Left post
4. Right post
5. Door

Close your eyes and walk through these five locations until you know them by heart. Make sure you remember that after you reach the porch, you turn to the left post first and then to the right post before moving to the door.

6-10

Now open the door and walk into the church. On the porch, you moved from left to right: left post to right post. Inside we'll do the same. First look left and slowly walk down the center aisle while looking to your left. Your next five locations are:

6. Back left pew
7. Back left window
8. Middle left pew
9. Front left window
10. Front left pew

Now you have walked up to the front of the center aisle and are ready for your next five locations.

11-15

Again, we will circle this area left to right, or in a clockwise direction.

11. Altar
12. Pulpit
13. Choir
14. Font
15. Piano

16-20

Now turn and walk back down the center aisle, looking at the other side of the room. Your next five locations are:

16. Front right pew
17. Front right window
18. Middle right pew
19. Back right window
20. Back right pew.

You're back to the door. But don't go through it. Let's be more creative.

21-25

Turn on your turbo power and rocket yourself directly up into the steeple! Here are your next five locations:

21. Steeple
22. Roof (now jump)
23. Grassy area to the left of the church
24. Sign
25. Parking area

26-30

Walk toward the parsonage for the last five locations:

26. Parsonage
27. Cemetery gate
28. Marble gravestone
29. Wood cross
30. Oak tree

How did you do? Check the schematic and paintings to review the journey locations.

Again, close your eyes and walk back through the church journey, stopping at each location in sets of five. Know this journey by heart before you move on to the next section.

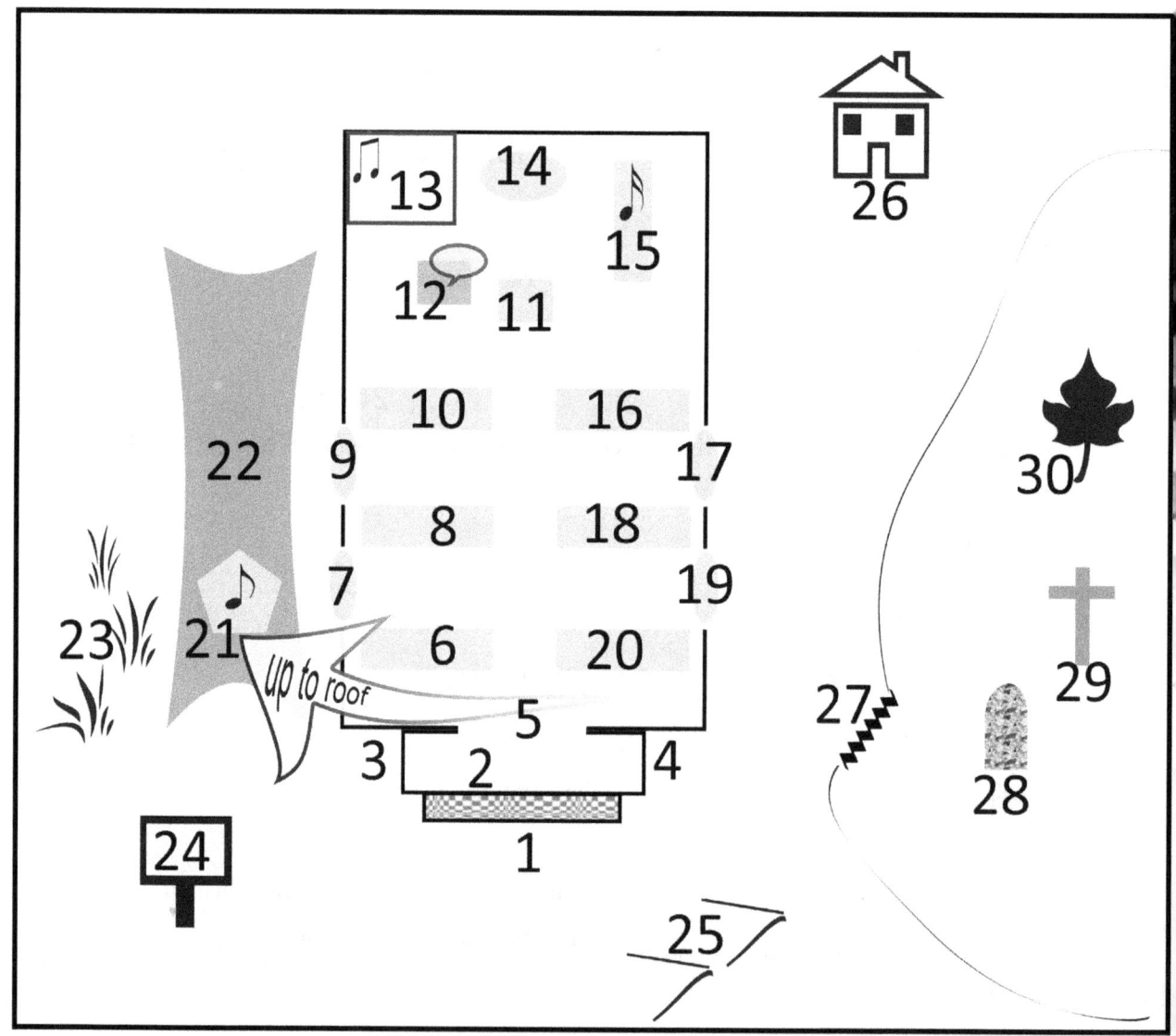

Parables Images: Seeing & Remembering

> *At its simplest, a parable is a metaphor or simile drawn from nature or common life, arresting the hearer by its vividness or strangeness, and leaving the mind in sufficient doubt about its precise application to tease it into active thought.*
>
> —C. H. Dodd

You may be thinking at this point: All this work, and I still haven't memorized the parables. Surprise! The hard part is over. Congratulations. Creating a memorable journey is most of the work. Now you just get to place interesting images along your journey. Specifically, one at a time, you will associate each parable with a symbol that reminds you of the parable, and you will place that symbol at its designated location along your journey.

Memorize Parable Titles

Begin by associating one simple image for each parable (a "title" or "name" image) along each location in your journey. We've given you a start by providing simple watercolor images that symbolize each parable. Use these to help you visualize a symbol to represent each parable. Feel free to make your own sketches. For the Great Fish parable, we saw a marlin. Perhaps you see a whale. Or perhaps you see the fisherman pulling in his net that contains mostly small fish and one great fish. Personalize your image.

Add Parable Details

What if you want to remember more details about the parable? For example, say you want to remember that the Lost Sheep parable not only involves a sheep (your "title" image), but also a shepherd, who is like the Kingdom. Instead of adding another figure to the symbol such as a shepherd or a king, just put a crown on the sheep. This will remind you that the shepherd represents the kingdom of heaven. Add details to your symbol so you remember all that you want to about that parable. Also, just by thinking about the parable and devising ways to represent it, that mental process alone will help you remember it. The point is, you're engaged. If you're engaged, interested, and want to remember—you will.

Fortunately, the parables are relatively simple in terms of characters, actions, events, and outcomes. But to help you see the essential details, we've distilled the parables into concise poems. Jesus didn't speak in 17th century English (the language of the King James Bible), so we want you to focus on the main events in each parable instead of getting caught up in a particular translation. Feel free to write your own poems to meditate on the essence of each parable. We won't interpret the parable. That's up to you. But we draw your attention to the symbols (or figurative language) Jesus used when he taught the parables.

> *If you want to remember courage, think of Ares and Achilles; or metalworking, of Hephaistos; or cowardice, of Epeios.*
>
> —the Dialexeis

> *We can recall a time from something coeval with it. Thus we recall April by flowers, Autumn from a winepress, and likewise for the other seasons.*
>
> —Giordano Bruno

1. *Sower*
2. *Seed Growing Secretly*
3. *Wicked Tenants*
4. *Budding Fig Tree*
5. *Leaven*
6. *Treasure*
7. *Pearl*
8. *Great Fish*
9. *Lost Sheep*
10. *Unforgiving Servant*
11. *Vineyard Workers*
12. *Two Sons*
13. *Lamps & Virgins*
14. *Talents*
15. *Wine Bottles*
16. *Good Samaritan*
17. *Friend at Midnight*
18. *Good Gifts*
19. *Rich Farmer*
20. *Thief*
21. *Barren Fig Tree*
22. *Mustard Seed*
23. *Great Supper*
24. *Tower Builder*
25. *Lost Coin*
26. *Prodigal Son*
27. *Unjust Steward*
28. *Rich Man & Lazarus*
29. *Unjust Judge*
30. *Pharisee & Publican*

Thirty Parables

Here we list the parables in the order in which they appear in Mark, Matthew, and Luke. The order isn't important, but some order is necessary for intentional remembering. In the next section, we meditate on each parable, one by one, with a poem and a painting. The painting helps you generate a symbolic image to represent the parable. The poem reminds you of what happens in the parable.

Take one parable at a time. See a symbolic image for the parable in the location on your journey. Move to the next parable. Take a break after every five parables to review.

In the following five pages, we provide a narrative to help you place and remember the titles of the 30 parables along the memory journey. To remember the names of the parables, simply move through the country church (or any other journey you choose). Adapt it to your personal vision. Although we provide details, be sure to stop and give each image your own details as well. Or create your own narrative and use our poems and paintings for assistance. If you're using our narrative, feel free to flip back and forth between the narrative and the poem-painting pages.

1. **Sower:** Begin at the steps outside and see a Sower scattering seeds.

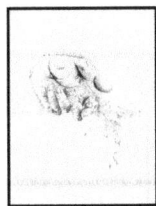

2. **Seed Growing Secretly:** Step up onto the church porch, look down, and see a trapdoor. Beneath the trapdoor see a seed growing secretly. Or maybe a tiny seedling pushes up through the porch floorboards.

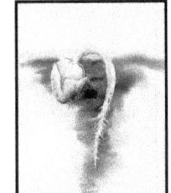

3. **Wicked Tenants:** Look to your left. Several wicked tenants are swinging around the left post. Do the tenants seem inappropriate at the entrance to the church? (Note that details are useful for helping you remember. The wilder the tenants look, the more likely you'll remember them.)

4. **Budding Fig Tree:** Look to your right; a young fig tree, leaning against the right post, is budding, promising future fruit.

5. **Leaven:** Step up to the door of the church where a woman is kneading bread. Ask yourself how you're going to get by her so you can enter the church.

This is your first group of five parables. Pause a moment to review them. Know them by heart before you move inside and start down the left side of the church.

6. **Treasure:** Look closely at the first pew. There's a treasure chest sitting on it. Open it. Dig your hands into the gold coins.

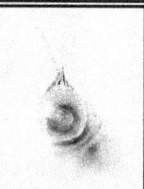
7. **Pearl:** Look up at the first window, or even better move over to it. Move your hand along the glass. Is the glass stained? Or simply transparent? See a pearl hanging from a chain sparkling in the window light.

8. **Great Fish:** The middle pew suddenly dissolves into water, and a great fish leaps out into a net that materializes beside the water.

9. **Lost Sheep:** The last window is open. Look out. See a handsome sheep walking alone across a distant meadow.

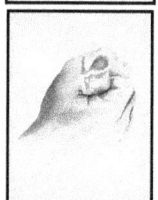
10. **Unforgiving Servant:** Sit for a moment on the front left pew. Beside you is an unforgiving servant holding his hand out, demanding payment. See his strong fist clench a ten-dollar bill.

Take a break. Know that you're at location number ten. Why is this place significant? Do you get annoyed by people demanding payment? Do you have bills to pay? Think about the ten-dollar bill you might owe the guy. Then move to the front of the church.

11. **Vineyard Workers:** At the altar see a vineyard worker cutting bunches of grapes or pruning a grapevine.

12. **Two Sons:** At the pulpit a father is kneeling, talking to his two sons.

13. **Lamps & Virgins:** In the left corner, a choir of young women sings harmoniously, each holding a lamp to see their music.

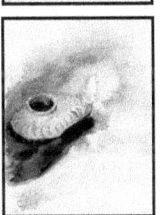

14. **Talents:** At the baptismal font, someone is tossing in talents (coins). See the person hand you some coins, a return on your investment.

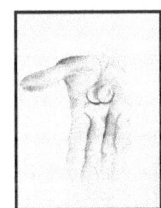

15. **Wine Bottles:** Someone has placed a wine bottle on the piano bench. The pianist picks it up and moves it to the floor before she starts playing.

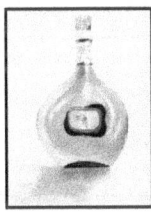

Rest. Think of a good symbol for the number 15. Put it on the piano bench with the pianist and the wine bottle. Then walk back through the church on the right side.

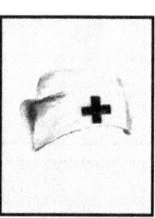
16. Good Samaritan: A man is lying on the pew closest to the piano. Someone, a Samaritan, is helping him up. Perhaps it's a nurse helping him. Or someone you know named Sam? Uncle Sam?

17. Friend at Midnight: Through the window nearest the front pew, a full moon shines, and you can just make out a friend of yours knocking on your door.

18. Good Gifts: Three beautifully wrapped Christmas gifts lie on the middle pew.

19. Rich Farmer: Looking out through the last window you see a farmer building a tremendously tall silo. He must be well-off and expects an abundant crop.

20. Thief: On the last pew a thief is moving toward the door. Did she steal something and is trying to escape? Or maybe she is hiding under the pew. Is she holding a twenty dollar bill? Or perhaps the thief looks funny because she's wearing a pair of eyeglasses to remind you that some people have 20-20 vision. Make this "20" image memorable.

Then rocket up into the steeple. You're turbo-charged.

21. **Barren Fig Tree:** As you pop out of the steeple you step on dead twigs and branches. Leaves have fallen to the gutters of the church. Then you see a barren fig tree growing out of the top of the steeple.

22. **Mustard Seed:** Carefully walk across the roof. Your foot slips, not because the roof is steep, but because the roof is covered in tiny brownish-gray mustard seeds. Look out! Use your balance.

23. **Great Supper:** Jump down to the grassy patch. Here women are preparing a good old country picnic. Smell the roast turkey sandwiches.

24. **Tower Builder:** Walk to the front exterior of the church. There you see a sign or a high ladder for installing a new sign. Or maybe it's not a ladder at all. Maybe the ladder grows into the Eiffel Tower! Paris! You imagine you've been there or want to go on your next vacation.

25. **Lost Coin:** To get a better view of the tower, walk into the parking lot. As you turn to look back, your foot scrapes something. What is it? A big shiny coin? Was this someone's offering that they dropped when they got out of the car to go into the church?

This is an easy spot to remember because it's location number 25. It's a 25-cent piece of silver. A big shiny quarter of silver like the U.S. used to make. Pick it up. Decide what you'll do next with the quarter. Then rest.

26. Prodigal Son: You're so proud of memorizing 25 of the parables that you decide to go tell the minister in his parsonage. Open the door and look inside. He greets you and calls you his prodigal son (or daughter). Or perhaps you see the minister's son, who is holding a shiny silver spoon.

27. Unjust Steward: At the gate to the cemetery, you see a steward dressed in fine black stewardly clothes, holding a clipboard with his to-do list. You assume he is coming to greet you. But instead, he turns his pockets out to show you that he is broke and has wasted his master's money. You wonder how that happened and ask him.

28. Rich Man & Lazarus: Standing on the marble gravestone is a rich, finely jeweled man. Gold ornaments spill from his pockets. Below him, kneeling on the ground, is Lazarus, looking deathly pale. When has he eaten last?

29. Unjust Judge: The wooden cross grave marker is taking a beating from a wooden gavel, belonging to a judge, who has apparently become frustrated by the appearance of a woman in his courtroom.

30. Pharisee & Publican: Anxious to rest and review your journey, you move to sit down under the old oak tree. There are two people already there: a stuffy Pharisee, thinking highly of himself, and a humble publican tax collector, bowing his head to the earth. Which one draws you?

Rest. Close your eyes. Go back to the beginning of your journey; step up to the church porch and start moving through your places slowly. See what's there and how much you remembered. Add details if you wish. Review until the parables enter your heart.

Once you know the parable titles by heart, use our poems and bible references to add details that remind you of additional aspects of the parable stories.

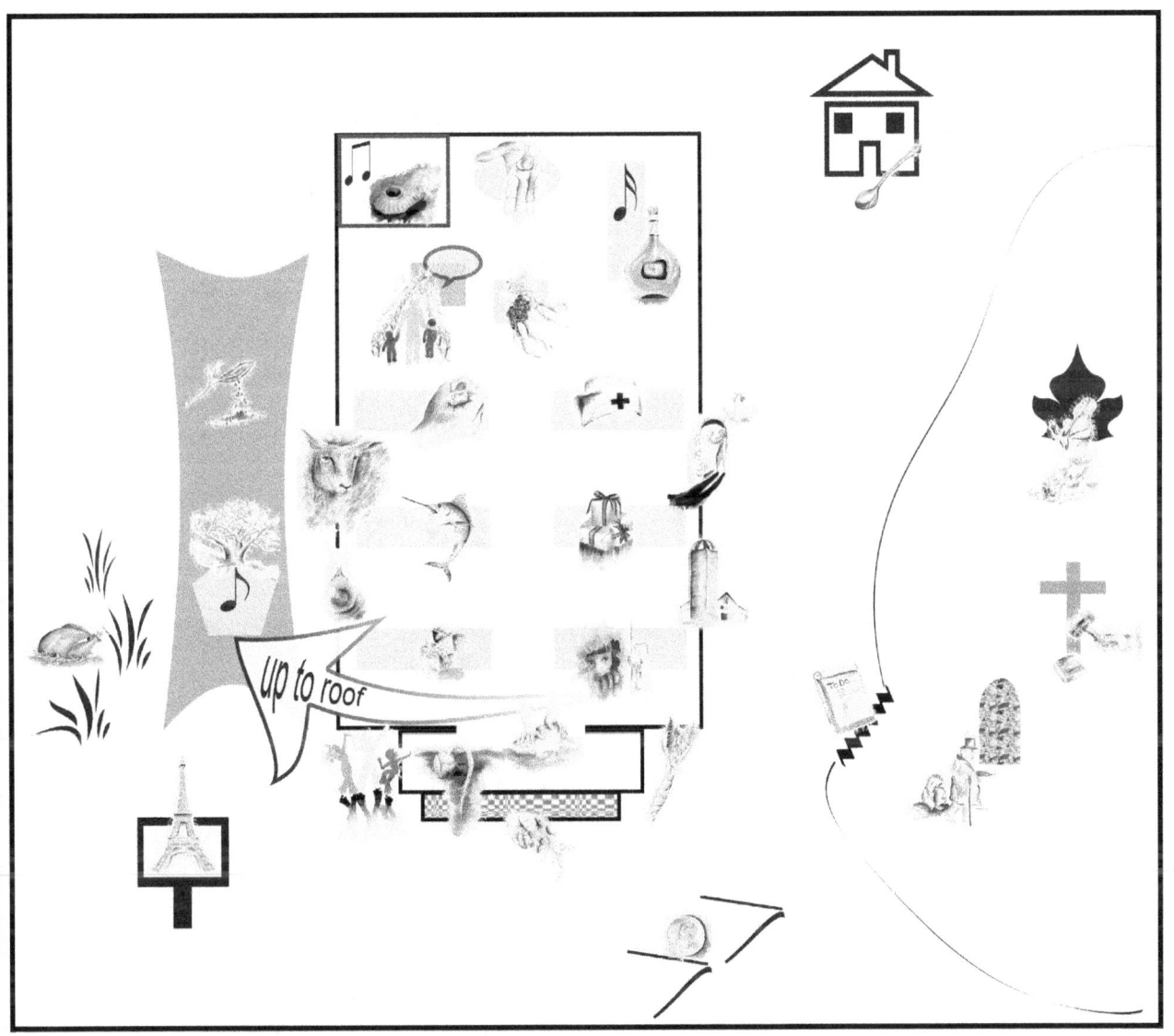

Poems & Paintings

The mules that angels ride come slowly down
The blazing passes, from beyond the sun.
Dissensions of their tinkling bells arrive.
These muleteers are dainty of their way.
Meantime, centurions guffaw and beat
Their shrilling tankards on the table-boards.
This parable, in sense, amounts to this:
The honey of heaven may or may not come,
But that of earth both comes and goes at once.
Suppose these couriers brought amid their train
A damsel heightened by eternal bloom.
—Wallace Stevens

Surely some revelation is at hand;
Surely the Second Coming is at hand.
The Second Coming! Hardly are those words out
When a vast image out of Spiritus Mundi
Troubles my sight: somewhere in sands of the desert
A shape with lion body and the head of a man...
—W. B. Yeats

Do not forget that a poem, even though it is composed in the language of information, is not used in the language-game of giving information.
—L. Wittgenstein

Sower

*A sower scatters seeds
his hands rough
from pulling weeds.*

*From here he says
you can imagine
the sea and see*

*the fishing boat.
Feel the warm breeze
when Jesus says*

*Look a sower went out
and scattered some seeds
and the first ones*

*were devoured by birds.
Others fell among stones
and had no depth to grow.*

*While others fell still
among thorns
and bore no fruit.*

*But blessed are you
and your ears
for they hear*

*and your eyes
for they see
the seeds that fill*

*good ground and produce
thirty, sixty, and one
hundred twenty per measure.*

Seed Growing Secretly

*A man casts a seed
in the kingdom of heaven.*

*The seed sprouts and grows
but how, he does not know.*

*It's a mystery of sleep
and rises while the earth*

*produces blade, ear, and corn
surprises that man reaps.*

Wicked Tenants

*Several wicked tenants dance
because a vineyard owner chanced
to lease them his vineyard
before he vanished.*

*Later the owner sent
his messenger for payment,
and the wicked tenants
laughed, caught, and beat him.*

*So the owner sent another
messenger and then another,
until the tenants even killed
his son, heir to the vineyard.*

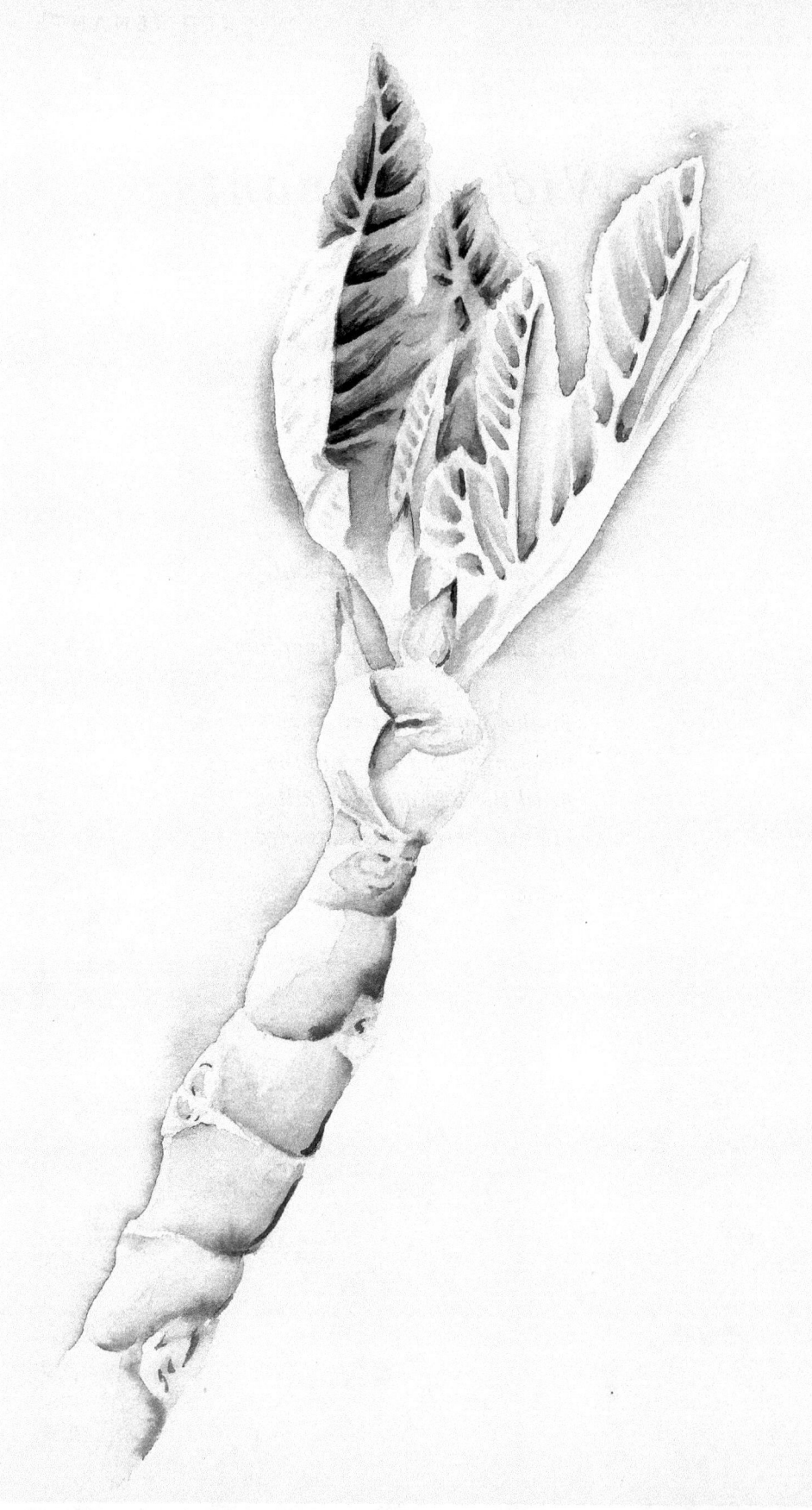

Budding Fig Tree

*When you see
a fig tree budding
you know the spirit*

*of summer coming
to lift its branches
higher and higher.*

Leaven

*A woman kneads bread
in three measures
of meal she hid*

*the kingdom of Heaven
which is like unto leaven
Jesus says.*

Treasure

A man finds
a treasure
in a field

and sells
everything
to buy that field.

Pearl

*The kingdom
of heaven
is like a merchant*

*who finds a pearl
and sells everything
to buy that pearl.*

Great Fish

*Someone draws
in her net
full of small fishes*

*and finds
among them
a great fish,*

*and she throws
the rest back
almost tipping*

*the boat as she
chooses that one fish
without regret.*

Lost Sheep

*Ninety-nine sheep
graze
on tender grass*

*as their shepherd
counts them,
finding one missing.*

*The kingdom
of heaven
is like that shepherd*

*who leaves
ninety-nine
to search*

*for one,
rejoicing when
he finds it.*

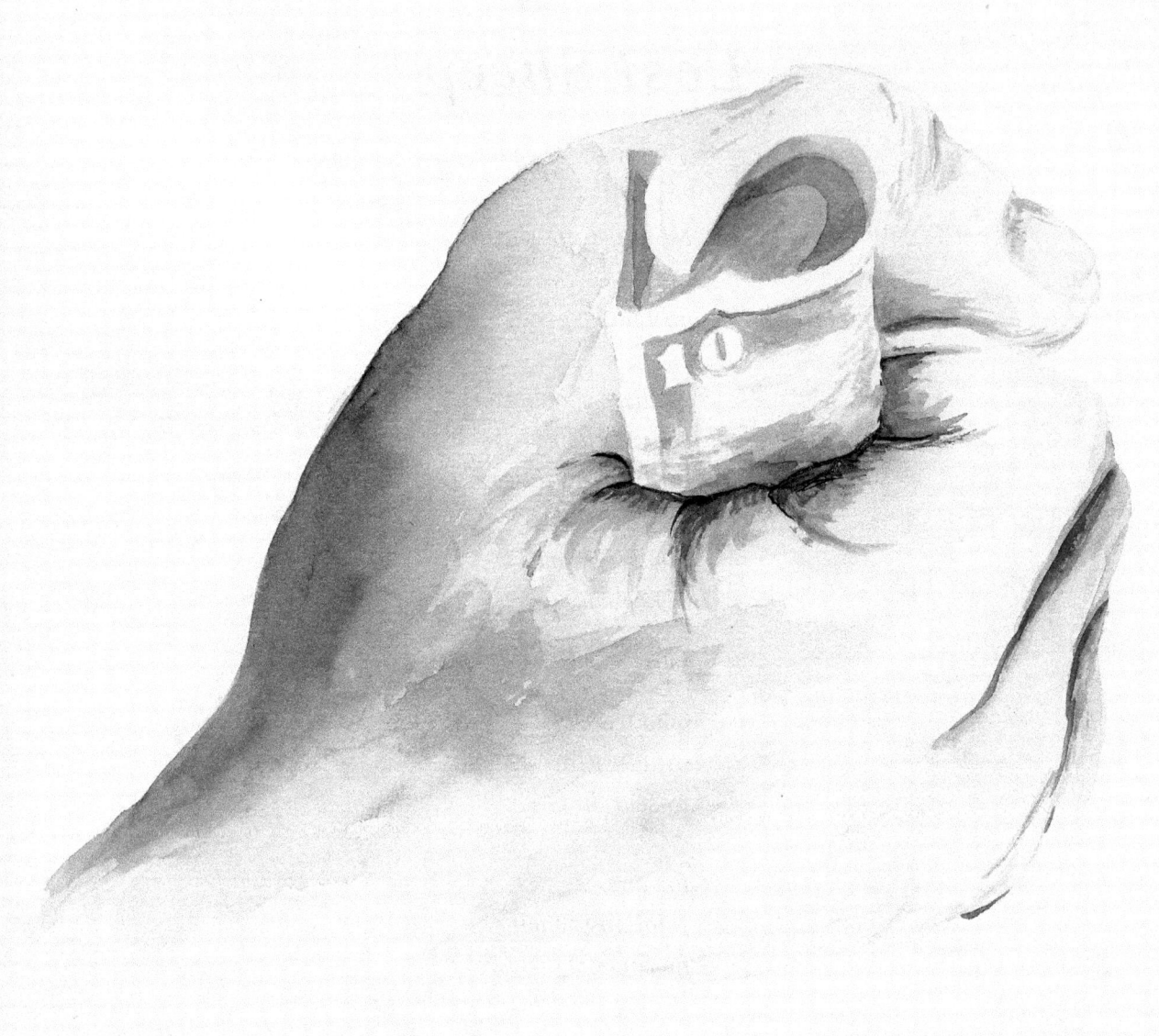

Unforgiving Servant

A servant pleads for a king's patience
concerning a debt the servant owes.

The kingdom of heaven is likened to this
compassionate king who forgives the servant.

But later the servant forgets to show compassion
and casts his own debtor into prison.

When the king finds out he delivers the servant
to his tormentors until he pays all that was owed.

Vineyard Workers

*The kingdom of heaven
is like a vineyard owner
who early one morning
hires workers who agree
to work all day for him.
About the third hour he
goes into the marketplace
and seeing others idle
hires them to work
for the same daily sum.
Then again he goes
at the sixth and the ninth
and even hires one
at the eleventh hour
for the same daily sum.*

*That evening he pays
as all had agreed upon
the same daily sum
which angers those
who came early.
But the owner says:
did you not
agree with me?
I have done no wrong.
Is it not my money?*

Two Sons

Among grapevines a father asks
his two sons to share a task.
One agrees but not the other,

and later his promise each
recants, acting like his brother.
Who has done the will of his father?

Lamps & Virgins

Ten virgins lit their lamps
to await the bridegroom
who was late coming.
While the bridegroom tarried
the virgins slumbered and slept.

Until a watcher at midnight
shouted: he arrives; he arrives;
go out to meet him.
And the ten virgins awoke
and trimmed their lamps.

Five had no oil left in their lamps,
and they had not brought extra.
So they asked the other five,
who had oil, for help. But they said:
no; we need it ourselves.

So the five virgins needing oil
hurried out to buy more,
making themselves foolishly late,
leaving only the wise virgins
to celebrate the marriage.

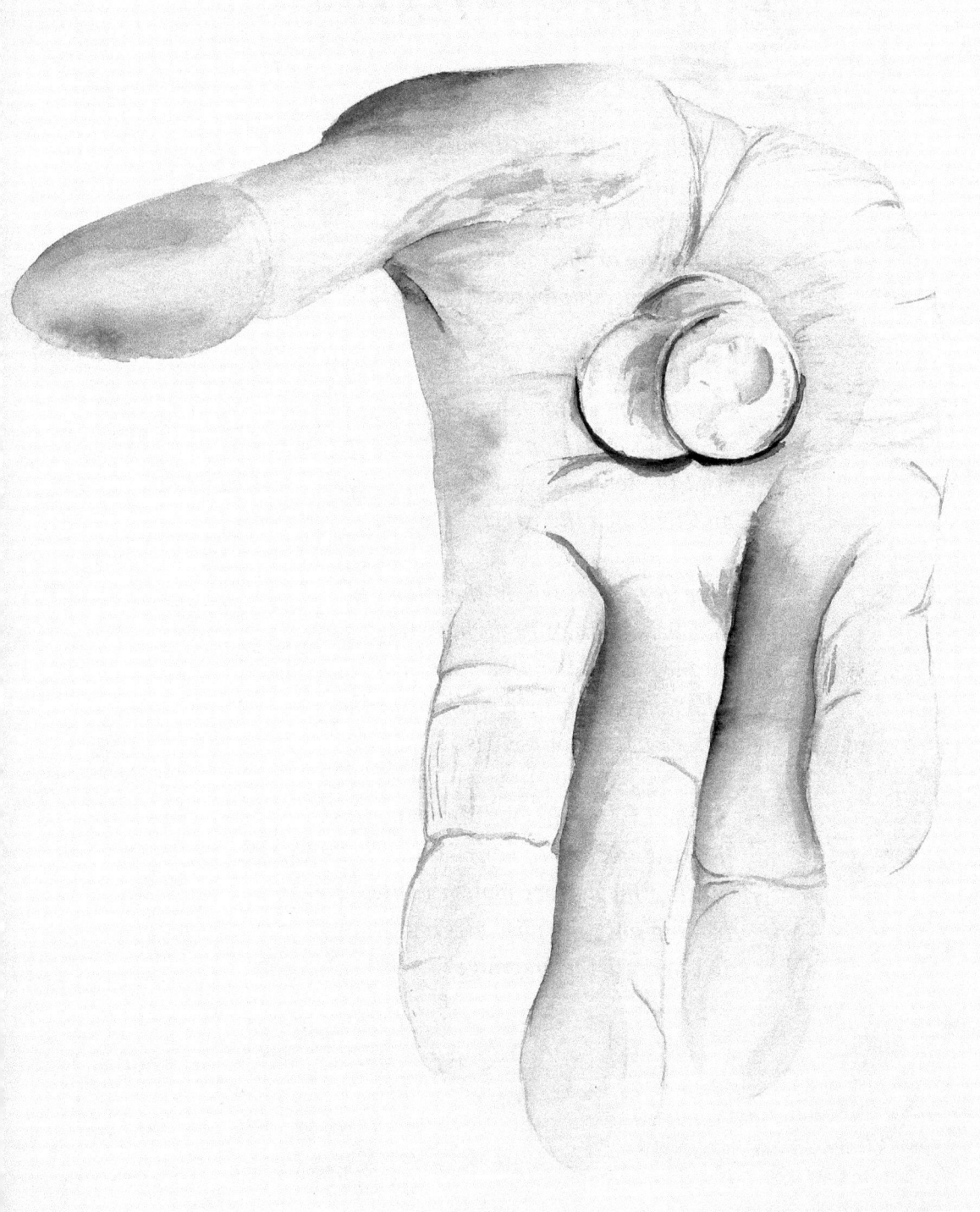

Talents

*A master entrusts money
to his servants before
leaving on a journey.*

*To one he gives five talents.
To a second he gives two.
And to one he gives one.*

*The three servants respond
according to themselves,
two invest, one buries.*

*When the master returns
he settles accounts
and the two who made*

*money he rewards,
but he takes the one
of the one who buried.*

Wine Bottles

*No one puts new wine in old
bottles or the bottles will burst.*

*And no one wants to drink old
wine from a new bottle.*

*But if new wine is put in new
bottles then both are preserved.*

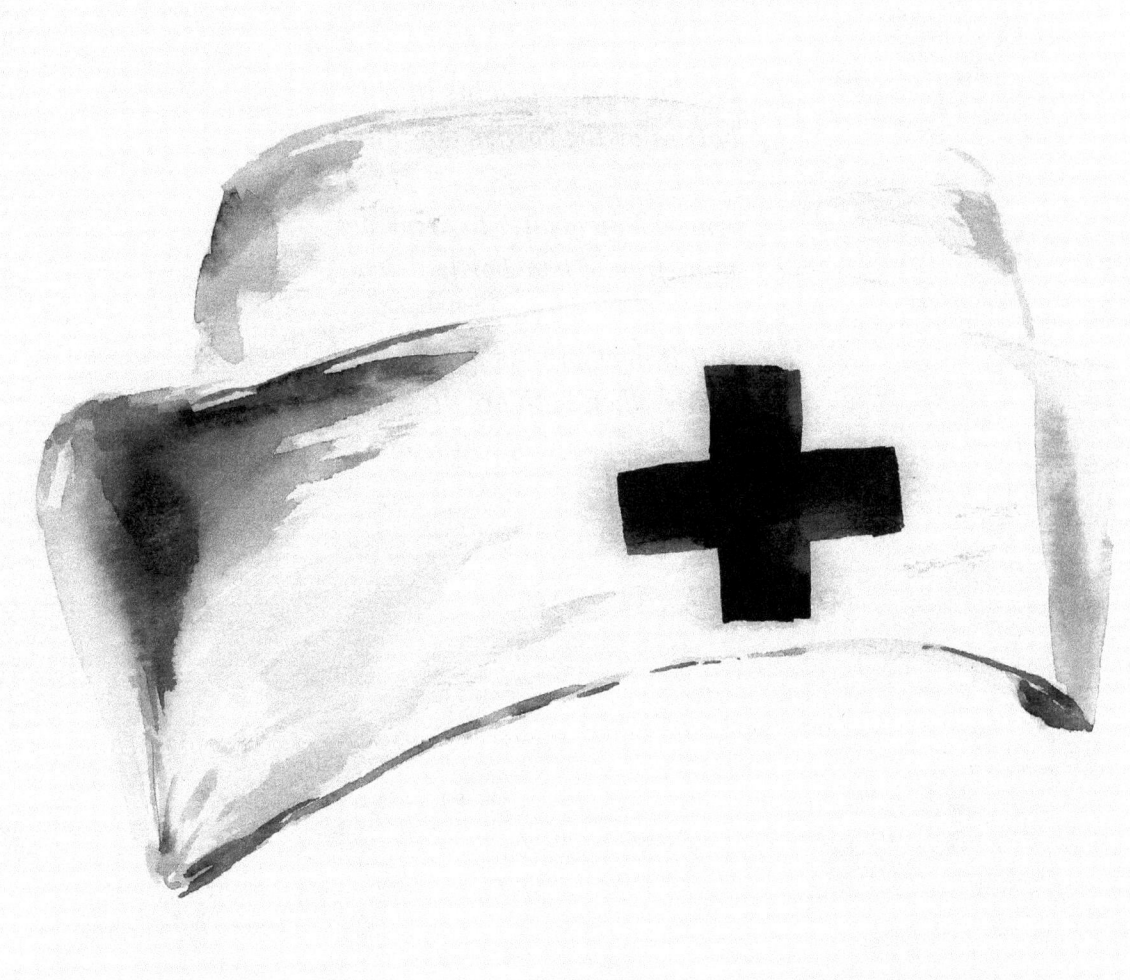

Good Samaritan

*A man fell among thieves
and as he lay dying
a priest and a Levite*

*by chance both respectable
men approached and seeing
him writhing passed heads*

*down onto the other side
leaving no traces. Then
a compassionate Samaritan*

*not normally favored in those
places happened by and bound
his wounds pouring oil and wine.*

Friend at Midnight

*At midnight a friend
calls on another friend
and asks for three loaves.*

*Does the friend open
the door even after
the lights are out?*

*Or does the friend say:
trouble me not;
don't you know the hour?*

Good Gifts

*Who among you when a son
asks for bread gives him a stone?*

*And who would hand a son
a snake if he asks for fish?*

*Surely you know to give
good gifts to your children.*

Rich Farmer

*A rich man tears down
his old barns to build
new bigger barns*

*and silos
to shelter his wealth;
then he dies unexpectedly.*

Thief

Blessed are those
with lights burning
who await someone

who is returning
from a wedding.
If a man knows

when a thief is coming
he waits, watches,
and his house is safe.

Barren Fig Tree

A fig tree
barely in leaf
bears no fruit

angering a man
who wants
to eat now

and threatens
to cut the tree down
as if that could help

but a gardener
knowing that
gardens and men

sleep and rise
requests time to hoe,
weed, and fertilize.

Mustard Seed

The kingdom of heaven is like a mustard
seed which a man casts into his garden

and it grows, becoming a tree
where the birds roost in its branches.

Great Supper

*The kingdom of heaven is like
a man who prepares a great supper
and sends his servants to say
my master invites you to his company.*

*One answers I have bills to pay.
One says I bought a house.
Another needs time to pray.
One sends his regrets*

*for someone he knows is departing.
So the man says to his servants: go to
the most unlikely places and gather
anyone you can. My house will be filled.*

Tower Builder

1.
A tower sways
above a war
going badly.

The tower was not
planned well and is
easy enough to mock.

2.
But the king waging war
reconsiders his odds
10 against 20

and sends his
ambassadors to negotiate
conditions for peace.

Lost Coin

*A woman who has ten
pieces of silver recounts
and finds only nine.*

*She lights a candle
to sweep her house
searching high*

*and low for the one
missing until
finding it*

*she cries out:
everyone come
and rejoice with me.*

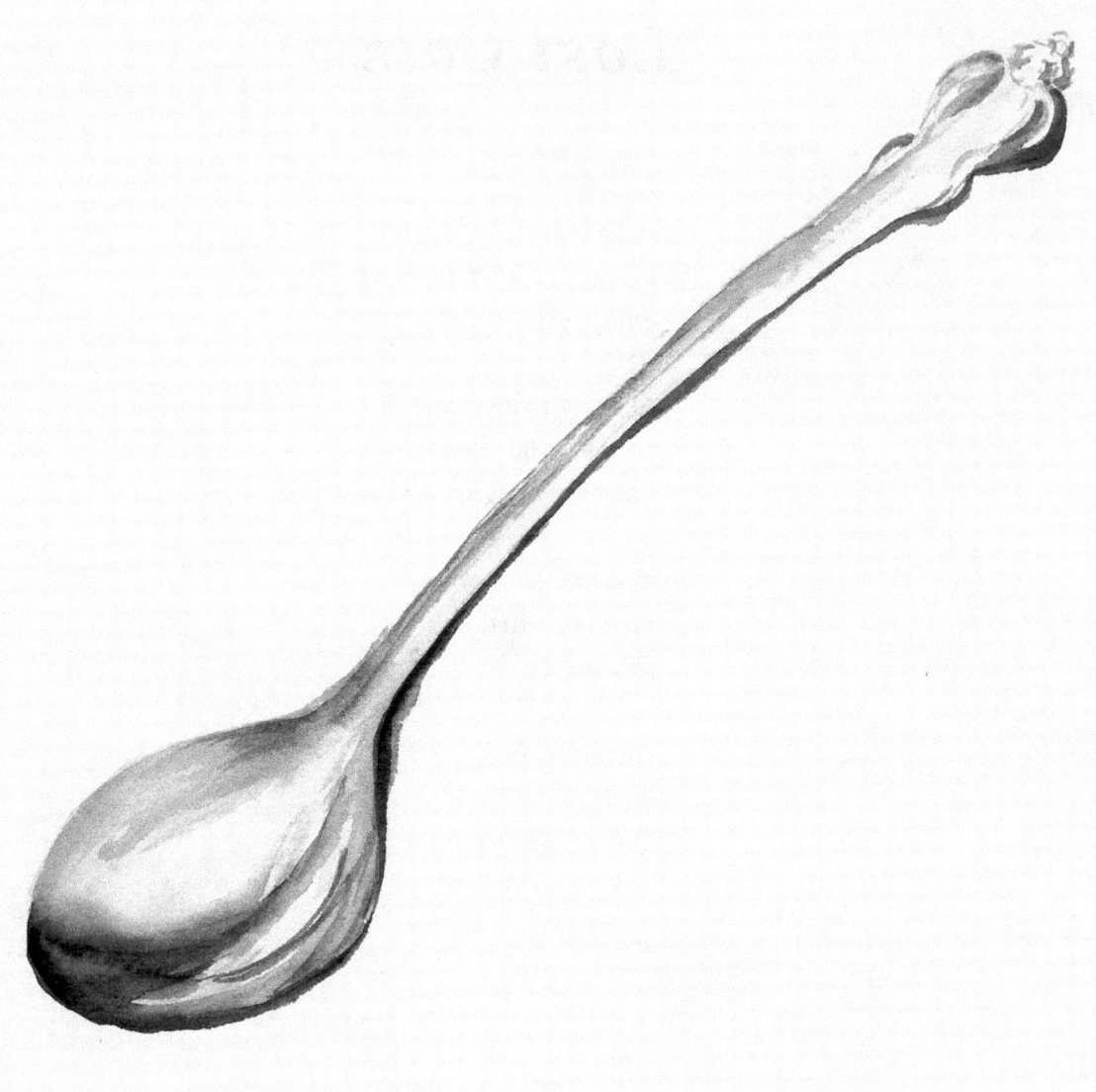

Prodigal Son

*Standing tall
the prodigal son
returns to his father*

*who, elated, hosts
a party and gives
that son his best robe*

*a ring and new clothes
angering his other son
who doesn't share*

*as trumpets blow
for others the joy
of his father*

*but the father says
be glad for your brother
for you the party is also.*

Unjust Steward

      1.
A rich man
fires his steward
for wasting money.

Distraught, the steward
endeavors to negotiate
with the rich man's debtors

and later is praised high
and low by the rich man
for behaving wisely.

      2.
One wonders
how we can
use the present

purposefully and
if that is a condition
for an enjoyable future.

Rich Man & Lazarus

*Lazarus lay at the gate of a rich man
who was clothed in fine purple linen.*

*The rich man fared sumptuously
while the dogs licked Lazarus' sores.*

*Then it came to pass that both men
died and nothing was as it was before.*

Unjust Judge

A judge presides
while a widow entreats
him to vindicate her
from an adversary.

He resists but she insists
until he is eventually
convinced by her rightful
case or persistence.

Pharisee & Publican

Two men went into the temple
one a Pharisee prayed
while the other a publican

several steps away
looked down and muttered
be merciful to me

while the Pharisee
said he was pleased
not to be like other men

including this nearby fellow.
Jesus says the man who
humbles himself will be exalted.

Parables in Matthew, Mark, Luke, & Thomas

Sower

Mark 4:3-8; Thomas 9

Mark 4

3: Hearken; Behold, there went out a sower to sow:

4: And it came to pass, as he sowed, some fell by the way side, and the fowls of the air came and devoured it up.

5: And some fell on stony ground, where it had not much earth; and immediately it sprang up, because it had no depth of earth:

6: But when the sun was up, it was scorched; and because it had no root, it withered away.

7: And some fell among thorns, and the thorns grew up, and choked it, and it yielded no fruit.

8: And other fell on good ground, and did yield fruit that sprang up and increased; and brought forth, some thirty, and some sixty, and some an hundred.

Thomas 9

Jesus said "Behold, he who sows came out, with his hand full of seeds and cast them onto the ground. Indeed, some did fall onto the road; where the birds came and consumed them. Some others fell onto rock and did not find root in the earth or send ears rising to the heavens. And some others did fall among thorns, which choked the seed, and were eaten by worms. Others yet still, did fall upon good earth and gave fruit up toward the heavens; and bore sixty per measure and one hundred and twenty per measure."

Seed Growing Secretly

Mark 4:26-29; Thomas 21

Mark 4

26: And he said, So is the kingdom of God, as if a man should cast seed into the ground;

27: And should sleep, and rise night and day, and the seed should spring and grow up, he knoweth not how.

28: For the earth bringeth forth fruit of herself; first the blade, then the ear, after that the full corn in the ear.

29: But when the fruit is brought forth, immediately he putteth in the sickle, because the harvest is come.

Thomas 21

Let there come to be among you a man of understanding. When the seed bears fruit, he will come quickly, sickle in hand to reap the harvest. Let he who has ears to listen, so listen."

Wicked Tenants

Mark 12:1-8; Matthew 21:33-39; Luke 20:9-15; Thomas 65

Mark 12

1: And he began to speak unto them by parables. A certain man planted a vineyard, and set an hedge about it, and digged a place for the winefat, and built a tower, and let it out to husbandmen, and went into a far country.
2: And at the season he sent to the husbandmen a servant, that he might receive from the husbandmen of the fruit of the vineyard.
3: And they caught him, and beat him, and sent him away empty.
4: And again he sent unto them another servant; and at him they cast stones, and wounded him in the head, and sent him away shamefully handled.
5: And again he sent another; and him they killed, and many others; beating some, and killing some.
6: Having yet therefore one son, his wellbeloved, he sent him also last unto them, saying, They will reverence my son.
7: But those husbandmen said among themselves, This is the heir; come, let us kill him, and the inheritance shall be ours.
8: And they took him, and killed him, and cast him out of the vineyard.

Matthew 21

33: Hear another parable: There was a certain householder, which planted a vineyard, and hedged it round about, and digged a winepress in it, and built a tower, and let it out to husbandmen, and went into a far country:
34: And when the time of the fruit drew near, he sent his servants to the husbandmen, that they might receive the fruits of it.
35: And the husbandmen took his servants, and beat one, and killed another, and stoned another.
36: Again, he sent other servants more than the first: and they did unto them likewise.
37: But last of all he sent unto them his son, saying, They will reverence my son.
38: But when the husbandmen saw the son, they said among themselves, This is the heir; come, let us kill him, and let us seize on his inheritance.
39: And they caught him, and cast him out of the vineyard, and slew him.

Luke 20

9: Then began he to speak to the people this parable; A certain man planted a vineyard, and let it forth to husbandmen, and went into a far country for a long time.
10: And at the season he sent a servant to the husbandmen, that they should give him of the fruit of the vineyard: but the husbandmen beat him, and sent him away empty.
11: And again he sent another servant: and they beat him also, and entreated him shamefully, and sent him away empty.
12: And again he sent a third: and they wounded him also, and cast him out.

13: Then said the lord of the vineyard, What shall I do? I will send my beloved son: it may be they will reverence him when they see him.

14: But when the husbandmen saw him, they reasoned among themselves, saying, This is the heir: come, let us kill him, that the inheritance may be ours.

15: So they cast him out of the vineyard, and killed him.

Thomas 65

Jesus said "A righteous man owned a vineyard. He put it in the charge of some tenants, so that they might work it for him, and that he might take his share of the harvest from their work. He sent his servant, so that the tenants might give him his share of the harvest from the vineyard. They took hold of his servant and beat him, almost to the point of death. The servant departed from that place and told his master. His master said "Perhaps they did not recognize him." He sent another servant, and the tenants beat this one too. Then the master sent his own son. He said "Perhaps they will show respect to my own son." Because the tenants who were there knew that this was the heir to the vineyard, they seized him and murdered him.

Budding Fig Tree

Mark 13:28-29; Matthew 24:32-34; Luke 21:29-32

Mark 13

28: Now learn a parable of the fig tree; When her branch is yet tender, and putteth forth leaves, ye know that summer is near:

29: So ye in like manner, when ye shall see these things come to pass, know that it is nigh, even at the doors.

Matthew 24

32: Now learn a parable of the fig tree; When his branch is yet tender, and putteth forth leaves, ye know that summer is nigh:

33: So likewise ye, when ye shall see all these things, know that it is near, even at the doors.

34: Verily I say unto you, This generation shall not pass, till all these things be fulfilled.

Luke 21

29: And he spake to them a parable; Behold the fig tree, and all the trees;

30: When they now shoot forth, ye see and know of your own selves that summer is now nigh at hand.

31: So likewise ye, when ye see these things come to pass, know ye that the kingdom of God is nigh at hand.

32: Verily I say unto you, This generation shall not pass away, till all be fulfilled.

Leaven

Matthew 13:33; Luke 13:20-21; Thomas 96

Matthew 13

33: Another parable spake he unto them; The kingdom of heaven is like unto leaven, which a woman took, and hid in three measures of meal, till the whole was leavened.

Luke 13
20: And again he said, Whereunto shall I liken the kingdom of God?
21: It is like leaven, which a woman took and hid in three measures of meal, till the whole was leavened.

Thomas 96
Jesus said "The Kingdom of the Father compares to a woman who took a little yeast, and put it into a dough and made it into some great loaves of bread."

Treasure

Matthew 13:44; Thomas 109

Matthew 13
44: Again, the kingdom of heaven is like unto treasure hid in a field; the which when a man hath found, he hideth, and for joy thereof goeth and selleth all that he hath, and buyeth that field.

Thomas 109
Jesus said "The Kingdom compares to a man who had in his field hidden treasure, and did not know anything about it, and after his death he left it to his son. Neither did the son know, he received the field and then sold it. When the person who bought it found it, he found the treasure.

Pearl

Matthew 13:45-46; Thomas 76

Matthew 13
45: Again, the kingdom of heaven is like unto a merchant man, seeking goodly pearls:
46: Who, when he had found one pearl of great price, went and sold all that he had, and bought it.

Thomas 76
Jesus said "The Kingdom of the Father compares to a trader who had some ordinary goods, but fell upon a pearl. The trader was a wise man, he gave the ordinary goods away and bought for himself the pearl alone."

Great Fish

Matthew 13:47-48; Thomas 8

Matthew 13
47: Again, the kingdom of heaven is like unto a net, that was cast into the sea, and gathered of every kind:
48: Which, when it was full, they drew to shore, and sat down, and gathered the good into vessels, but cast the bad away.

Thomas 8
And he said "The man does compare to a wise fisherman, the one who cast his nets into the sea and drew it up from the sea, full of small fish from the depths. Amongst these the wise fisherman found a large fish; so he cast all the small fish back into the sea and chose the large fish without difficulty."

Lost Sheep

Matthew 18:12-13; Luke 15:4-6; Thomas 107

Matthew 18

12: How think ye? if a man have an hundred sheep, and one of them be gone astray, doth he not leave the ninety and nine, and goeth into the mountains, and seeketh that which is gone astray?

13: And if so be that he find it, verily I say unto you, he rejoiceth more of that sheep, than of the ninety and nine which went not astray.

Luke 15

4: What man of you, having an hundred sheep, if he lose one of them, doth not leave the ninety and nine in the wilderness, and go after that which is lost, until he find it?

5: And when he hath found it, he layeth it on his shoulders, rejoicing.

6: And when he cometh home, he calleth together his friends and neighbors, saying unto them, Rejoice with me; for I have found my sheep which was lost.

Thomas 107

Jesus said "The Kingdom compares to a man herding sheep, who had there with him one hundred sheep. One of them did stray, the largest one. He left the other ninety-nine and searched for the one he had lost, until he found it. He said to this sheep "I love you more than the other ninety nine."

Unforgiving Servant

Matthew 18:23-34

Matthew 18

23: Therefore is the kingdom of heaven likened unto a certain king, which would take account of his servants.

24: And when he had begun to reckon, one was brought unto him, which owed him ten thousand talents.

25: But forasmuch as he had not to pay, his lord commanded him to be sold, and his wife, and children, and all that he had, and payment to be made.

26: The servant therefore fell down, and worshipped him, saying, Lord, have patience with me, and I will pay thee all.

27: Then the lord of that servant was moved with compassion, and loosed him, and forgave him the debt.

28: But the same servant went out, and found one of his fellow servants, which owed him an hundred pence: and he laid hands on him, and took him by the throat, saying, Pay me that thou owest.

29: And his fellow servant fell down at his feet, and besought him, saying, Have patience with me, and I will pay thee all.

30: And he would not: but went and cast him into prison, till he should pay the debt.

31: So when his fellow servants saw what was done, they were very sorry, and came and told unto their lord all that was done.

32: Then his lord, after that he had called

him, said unto him, O thou wicked servant, I forgave thee all that debt, because thou desiredst me:

33: Shouldest not thou also have had compassion on thy fellow servant, even as I had pity on thee?

34: And his lord was wroth, and delivered him to the tormentors, till he should pay all that was due unto him.

Vineyard Workers

Matthew 20:1-15

Matthew 20

1: For the kingdom of heaven is like unto a man that is an householder, which went out early in the morning to hire laborers into his vineyard.

2: And when he had agreed with the laborers for a penny a day, he sent them into his vineyard.

3: And he went out about the third hour, and saw others standing idle in the marketplace,

4: And said unto them; Go ye also into the vineyard, and whatsoever is right I will give you. And they went their way.

5: Again he went out about the sixth and ninth hour, and did likewise.

6: And about the eleventh hour he went out, and found others standing idle, and saith unto them, Why stand ye here all the day idle?

7: They say unto him, Because no man hath hired us. He saith unto them, Go ye also into the vineyard; and whatsoever is right, that shall ye receive.

8: So when even was come, the lord of the vineyard saith unto his steward, Call the laborers, and give them their hire, beginning from the last unto the first.

9: And when they came that were hired about the eleventh hour, they received every man a penny.

10: But when the first came, they supposed that they should have received more; and they likewise received every man a penny.

11: And when they had received it, they murmured against the good man of the house,

12: Saying, These last have wrought but one hour, and thou hast made them equal unto us, which have borne the burden and heat of the day.

13: But he answered one of them, and said, Friend, I do thee no wrong: didst not thou agree with me for a penny?

14: Take that thine is, and go thy way: I will give unto this last, even as unto thee.

15: Is it not lawful for me to do what I will with mine own? Is thine eye evil, because I am good?

Two Sons

Matthew 21:28-31

Matthew 21

28: But what think ye? A certain man had two sons; and he came to the first, and said, Son, go work to day in my vineyard.

29: He answered and said, I will not: but afterward he repented, and went.
30: And he came to the second, and said likewise. And he answered and said, I go, sir: and went not.
31: Whether of them twain did the will of his father? They say unto him, The first. Jesus saith unto them, Verily I say unto you, That the publicans and the harlots go into the kingdom of God before you.

Lamps & Virgins

Matthew 25:1-12

Matthew 25

1: Then shall the kingdom of heaven be likened unto ten virgins, which took their lamps, and went forth to meet the bridegroom.
2: And five of them were wise, and five were foolish.
3: They that were foolish took their lamps, and took no oil with them:
4: But the wise took oil in their vessels with their lamps.
5: While the bridegroom tarried, they all slumbered and slept.
6: And at midnight there was a cry made, Behold, the bridegroom cometh; go ye out to meet him.
7: Then all those virgins arose, and trimmed their lamps.
8: And the foolish said unto the wise, Give us of your oil; for our lamps are gone out.
9: But the wise answered, saying, Not so; lest there be not enough for us and you: but go ye rather to them that sell, and buy for yourselves.
10: And while they went to buy, the bridegroom came; and they that were ready went in with him to the marriage: and the door was shut.
11: Afterward came also the other virgins, saying, Lord, Lord, open to us.
12: But he answered and said, Verily I say unto you, I know you not.

Talents

Matthew 25:14-29; Luke 19:11-27

Matthew 25

14: For the kingdom of heaven is as a man travelling into a far country, who called his own servants, and delivered unto them his goods.
15: And unto one he gave five talents, to another two, and to another one; to every man according to his several ability; and straightway took his journey.
16: Then he that had received the five talents went and traded with the same, and made them other five talents.
17: And likewise he that had received two, he also gained other two.
18: But he that had received one went and digged in the earth, and hid his lord's money.
19: After a long time the lord of those servants cometh, and reckoneth with them.

20: And so he that had received five talents came and brought other five talents, saying, Lord, thou deliveredst unto me five talents: behold, I have gained beside them five talents more.
21: His lord said unto him, Well done, thou good and faithful servant: thou hast been faithful over a few things, I will make thee ruler over many things: enter thou into the joy of thy lord.
22: He also that had received two talents came and said, Lord, thou deliveredst unto me two talents: behold, I have gained two other talents beside them.
23: His lord said unto him, Well done, good and faithful servant; thou hast been faithful over a few things, I will make thee ruler over many things: enter thou into the joy of thy lord.
24: Then he which had received the one talent came and said, Lord, I knew thee that thou art an hard man, reaping where thou hast not sown, and gathering where thou hast not strawed:
25: And I was afraid, and went and hid thy talent in the earth: lo, there thou hast that is thine.
26: His lord answered and said unto him, Thou wicked and slothful servant, thou knewest that I reap where I sowed not, and gather where I have not strawed:
27: Thou oughtest therefore to have put my money to the exchangers, and then at my coming I should have received mine own with usury.
28: Take therefore the talent from him, and give it unto him which hath ten talents.
29: For unto every one that hath shall be given, and he shall have abundance: but from him that hath not shall be taken away even that which he hath.

Luke 19

11: And as they heard these things, he added and spake a parable, because he was nigh to Jerusalem, and because they thought that the kingdom of God should immediately appear.
12: He said therefore, A certain nobleman went into a far country to receive for himself a kingdom, and to return.
13: And he called his ten servants, and delivered them ten pounds, and said unto them, Occupy till I come.
14: But his citizens hated him, and sent a message after him, saying, We will not have this man to reign over us.
15: And it came to pass, that when he was returned, having received the kingdom, then he commanded these servants to be called unto him, to whom he had given the money, that he might know how much every man had gained by trading.
16: Then came the first, saying, Lord, thy pound hath gained ten pounds.
17: And he said unto him, Well, thou good servant: because thou hast been faithful in a very little, have thou authority over ten cities.
18: And the second came, saying, Lord, thy pound hath gained five pounds.
19: And he said likewise to him, Be thou also

over five cities.

20: And another came, saying, Lord, behold, here is thy pound, which I have kept laid up in a napkin:

21: For I feared thee, because thou art an austere man: thou takest up that thou layedst not down, and reapest that thou didst not sow.

22: And he saith unto him, Out of thine own mouth will I judge thee, thou wicked servant. Thou knewest that I was an austere man, taking up that I laid not down, and reaping that I did not sow:

23: Wherefore then gavest not thou my money into the bank, that at my coming I might have required mine own with usury?

24: And he said unto them that stood by, Take from him the pound, and give it to him that hath ten pounds.

25: (And they said unto him, Lord, he hath ten pounds.)

26: For I say unto you, That unto every one which hath shall be given; and from him that hath not, even that he hath shall be taken away from him.

27: But those mine enemies, which would not that I should reign over them, bring hither, and slay them before me.

Wine Bottles

Luke 5:37-39; Matthew 9:16-17; Mark 2:21-22; Thomas 47

Luke 5

37: And no man putteth new wine into old bottles; else the new wine will burst the bottles, and be spilled, and the bottles shall perish.

38: But new wine must be put into new bottles; and both are preserved.

39: No man also having drunk old wine straightway desireth new.

Matthew 9

16: No man putteth a piece of new cloth unto an old garment, for that which is put in to fill it up taketh from the garment, and the rent is made worse.

17: Neither do men put new wine into old bottles: else the bottles break, and the wine runneth out, and the bottles perish: but they put new wine into new bottles, and both are preserved.

Mark 2

21: No man also seweth a piece of new cloth on an old garment: else the new piece that filled it up taketh away from the old, and the rent is made worse.

22: And no man putteth new wine into old bottles: else the new wine doth burst the bottles, and the wine is spilled, and the bottles will be marred: but new wine must be put into new bottles.

Thomas 47

Jesus said "No man drinks old wine and immediately desires to drink new wine. And they do not pour new wine into old wine skins, otherwise they would split open. Nor do they pour old wine into new wineskin otherwise it would spoil."

Good Samaritan

Luke 10:30-36

Luke 10

30: And Jesus answering said, A certain man went down from Jerusalem to Jericho, and fell among thieves, which stripped him of his raiment, and wounded him, and departed, leaving him half dead.
31: And by chance there came down a certain priest that way: and when he saw him, he passed by on the other side.
32: And likewise a Levite, when he was at the place, came and looked on him, and passed by on the other side.
33: But a certain Samaritan, as he journeyed, came where he was: and when he saw him, he had compassion on him,
34: And went to him, and bound up his wounds, pouring in oil and wine, and set him on his own beast, and brought him to an inn, and took care of him.
35: And on the morrow when he departed, he took out two pence, and gave them to the host, and said unto him, Take care of him; and whatsoever thou spendest more, when I come again, I will repay thee.
36: Which now of these three, thinkest thou, was neighbor unto him that fell among the thieves?

Friend at Midnight

Luke 11:5-8

Luke 11

5: And he said unto them, Which of you shall have a friend, and shall go unto him at midnight, and say unto him, Friend, lend me three loaves;
6: For a friend of mine in his journey is come to me, and I have nothing to set before him?
7: And he from within shall answer and say, Trouble me not: the door is now shut, and my children are with me in bed; I cannot rise and give thee.
8: I say unto you, Though he will not rise and give him, because he is his friend, yet because of his importunity he will rise and give him as many as he needeth.

Good Gifts

Luke 11:11-13; Matthew 7: 9-11

Luke 11

11: If a son shall ask bread of any of you that is a father, will he give him a stone? or if he ask a fish, will he for a fish give him a serpent?
12: Or if he shall ask an egg, will he offer him a scorpion?
13: If ye then, being evil, know how to give good gifts unto your children: how much more shall your heavenly Father give the Holy Spirit to them that ask him?

Matthew 7

9: Or what man is there of you, whom if his son ask bread, will he give him a stone?
10: Or if he ask a fish, will he give him a

serpent?

11: If ye then, being evil, know how to give good gifts unto your children, how much more shall your Father which is in heaven give good things to them that ask him?

Rich Farmer

Luke 12:16-20; Thomas 63

Luke 12

16: And he spake a parable unto them, saying, The ground of a certain rich man brought forth plentifully:
17: And he thought within himself, saying, What shall I do, because I have no room where to bestow my fruits?
18: And he said, This will I do: I will pull down my barns, and build greater; and there will I bestow all my fruits and my goods.
19: And I will say to my soul, Soul, thou hast much goods laid up for many years; take thine ease, eat, drink, and be merry.
20: But God said unto him, Thou fool, this night thy soul shall be required of thee: then whose shall those things be, which thou hast provided?

Thomas 63

Jesus said "There was a rich man who had many riches. He said "I will make use of my riches, so that I may sow, reap and plant, and fill my storehouse with harvest, so that I will not be in need of anything." These were the thoughts in his mind, but during the night he died.

Thief

Luke 12:35-40; Thomas 21

Luke 12

35: Let your loins be girded about, and your lights burning;
36: And ye yourselves like unto men that wait for their lord, when he will return from the wedding; that when he cometh and knocketh, they may open unto him immediately.
37: Blessed are those servants, whom the lord when he cometh shall find watching: verily I say unto you, that he shall gird himself, and make them to sit down to meat, and will come forth and serve them.
38: And if he shall come in the second watch, or come in the third watch, and find them so, blessed are those servants.
39: And this know, that if the good man of the house had known what hour the thief would come, he would have watched, and not have suffered his house to be broken through.
40: Be ye therefore ready also: for the Son of man cometh at an hour when ye think not.

Thomas 21

Therefore I teach of it thus, if the owner of the house should realize that a thief is coming, he will keep watch before he comes, in order to prevent him from breaking into his house to steal his possessions. All of you therefore, keep watch against the world. Prepare yourselves with great power, so that the thieves are not able to find a way to get to you, because the persecutions you expect will surely come.

Barren Fig Tree

Luke 13:6-9

Luke 13
6: He spake also this parable; A certain man had a fig tree planted in his vineyard; and he came and sought fruit thereon, and found none.
7: Then said he unto the dresser of his vineyard, Behold, these three years I come seeking fruit on this fig tree, and find none: cut it down; why cumbereth it the ground?
8: And he answering said unto him, Lord, let it alone this year also, till I shall dig about it, and dung it:
9: And if it bear fruit, well: and if not, then after that thou shalt cut it down.

Mustard Seed

Luke 13:18-19; Matthew 13:31-32; Mark 4:30-32; Thomas 20

Luke 13
18: Then said he, Unto what is the kingdom of God like? and whereunto shall I resemble it?
19: It is like a grain of mustard seed, which a man took, and cast into his garden; and it grew, and waxed a great tree; and the fowls of the air lodged in the branches of it.

Matthew 13
31: Another parable put he forth unto them, saying, The kingdom of heaven is like to a grain of mustard seed, which a man took, and sowed in his field:
32: Which indeed is the least of all seeds: but when it is grown, it is the greatest among herbs, and becometh a tree, so that the birds of the air come and lodge in the branches thereof.

Mark 4
30: And he said, Whereunto shall we liken the kingdom of God? or with what comparison shall we compare it?
31: It is like a grain of mustard seed, which, when it is sown in the earth, is less than all the seeds that be in the earth:
32: But when it is sown, it groweth up, and becometh greater than all herbs, and shooteth out great branches; so that the fowls of the air may lodge under the shadow of it.

Thomas 20
The disciples said to him "Tell us! To what does the Kingdom of Heaven compare?" He said "It compares to a grain of mustard, smallest of all the seeds. When however it should fall onto worked ground, it does send forth mighty branches, which come to be a shelter for the birds of the sky."

Great Supper

Luke 14:16-23; Matthew 22:1-10; Thomas 64

Luke 14

16: Then said he unto him, A certain man made a great supper, and bade many:

17: And sent his servant at supper time to say to them that were bidden, Come; for all things are now ready.

18: And they all with one consent began to make excuse. The first said unto him, I have bought a piece of ground, and I must needs go and see it: I pray thee have me excused.

19: And another said, I have bought five yoke of oxen, and I go to prove them: I pray thee have me excused.

20: And another said, I have married a wife, and therefore I cannot come.

21: So that servant came, and shewed his lord these things. Then the master of the house being angry said to his servant, Go out quickly into the streets and lanes of the city, and bring in hither the poor, and the maimed, and the halt, and the blind.

22: And the servant said, Lord, it is done as thou hast commanded, and yet there is room.

23: And the lord said unto the servant, Go out into the highways and hedges, and compel them to come in, that my house may be filled.

Matthew 22

1: And Jesus answered and spake unto them again by parables, and said,

2: The kingdom of heaven is like unto a certain king, which made a marriage for his son,

3: And sent forth his servants to call them that were bidden to the wedding: and they would not come.

4: Again, he sent forth other servants, saying, Tell them which are bidden, Behold, I have prepared my dinner: my oxen and my fatlings are killed, and all things are ready: come unto the marriage.

5: But they made light of it, and went their ways, one to his farm, another to his merchandise:

6: And the remnant took his servants, and entreated them spitefully, and slew them.

7: But when the king heard thereof, he was wroth: and he sent forth his armies, and destroyed those murderers, and burned up their city.

8: Then saith he to his servants, The wedding is ready, but they which were bidden were not worthy.

9: Go ye therefore into the highways, and as many as ye shall find, bid to the marriage.

10: So those servants went out into the highways, and gathered together all as many as they found, both bad and good: and the wedding was furnished with guests.

Thomas 64

Jesus said "A man was having some visitors, and when he had prepared the feast, he sent his servant to call the visitors. He went to the first, and said "My master calls you." He replied, "I have to pay some traders who are coming to me this evening, for some orders I have placed with them. I must therefore be excused." The servant went to another one, and said to him "My master calls you." He replied, "My friend is getting married, and I must be the host so I cannot come. I must therefore be excused." He went up to another one, and said "My master calls you." He replied "I have bought this farm, and must go and collect what I am owed upon it. I must therefore be excused." The servant then came to his master and said "Those who you have called to the feast have all declined to come." The master said to his servant "Go outside, to the roads and call those who you see, so that they may feast. The buyers and the traders may not go into the places of my father."

Tower Builder

Luke 14:28-32

Luke 14

28: For which of you, intending to build a tower, sitteth not down first, and counteth the cost, whether he have sufficient to finish it?
29: Lest haply, after he hath laid the foundation, and is not able to finish it, all that behold it begin to mock him,
30: Saying, This man began to build, and was not able to finish.
31: Or what king, going to make war against another king, sitteth not down first, and consulteth whether he be able with ten thousand to meet him that cometh against him with twenty thousand?
32: Or else, while the other is yet a great way off, he sendeth an ambassage, and desireth conditions of peace.

Lost Coin

Luke 15:8-9

Luke 15

8: Either what woman having ten pieces of silver, if she lose one piece, doth not light a candle, and sweep the house, and seek diligently till she find it?
9: And when she hath found it, she calleth her friends and her neighbors together, saying, Rejoice with me; for I have found the piece which I had lost.

Prodigal Son

Luke 15:11-32

Luke 15

11: And he said, A certain man had two sons:
12: And the younger of them said to his father, Father, give me the portion of goods that falleth to me. And he divided unto them his living.
13: And not many days after the younger son gathered all together, and took his journey into a far country, and there wasted his substance with riotous living.
14: And when he had spent all, there arose a mighty famine in that land; and he began to be in want.
15: And he went and joined himself to a citizen of that country; and he sent him into

his fields to feed swine.

16: And he would fain have filled his belly with the husks that the swine did eat: and no man gave unto him.

17: And when he came to himself, he said, How many hired servants of my father's have bread enough and to spare, and I perish with hunger!

18: I will arise and go to my father, and will say unto him, Father, I have sinned against heaven, and before thee,

19: And am no more worthy to be called thy son: make me as one of thy hired servants.

20: And he arose, and came to his father. But when he was yet a great way off, his father saw him, and had compassion, and ran, and fell on his neck, and kissed him.

21: And the son said unto him, Father, I have sinned against heaven, and in thy sight, and am no more worthy to be called thy son.

22: But the father said to his servants, Bring forth the best robe, and put it on him; and put a ring on his hand, and shoes on his feet:

23: And bring hither the fatted calf, and kill it; and let us eat, and be merry:

24: For this my son was dead, and is alive again; he was lost, and is found. And they began to be merry.

25: Now his elder son was in the field: and as he came and drew nigh to the house, he heard musick and dancing.

26: And he called one of the servants, and asked what these things meant.

27: And he said unto him, Thy brother is come; and thy father hath killed the fatted calf, because he hath received him safe and sound.

28: And he was angry, and would not go in: therefore came his father out, and intreated him.

29: And he answering said to his father, Lo, these many years do I serve thee, neither transgressed I at any time thy commandment: and yet thou never gavest me a kid, that I might make merry with my friends:

30: But as soon as this thy son was come, which hath devoured thy living with harlots, thou hast killed for him the fatted calf.

31: And he said unto him, Son, thou art ever with me, and all that I have is thine.

32: It was meet that we should make merry, and be glad: for this thy brother was dead, and is alive again; and was lost, and is found.

Unjust Steward

Luke 16:1-8

Luke 16

1: And he said also unto his disciples, There was a certain rich man, which had a steward; and the same was accused unto him that he had wasted his goods.

2: And he called him, and said unto him, How is it that I hear this of thee? give an account of thy stewardship; for thou mayest be no longer steward.

3: Then the steward said within himself, What shall I do? for my lord taketh away from me the stewardship: I cannot dig; to beg I am ashamed.

4: I am resolved what to do, that, when I am put out of the stewardship, they may receive me into their houses.

5: So he called every one of his lord's debtors unto him, and said unto the first, How much owest thou unto my lord?

6: And he said, An hundred measures of oil. And he said unto him, Take thy bill, and sit down quickly, and write fifty.

7: Then said he to another, And how much owest thou? And he said, An hundred measures of wheat. And he said unto him, Take thy bill, and write fourscore.

8: And the lord commended the unjust steward, because he had done wisely.

Rich Man & Lazarus

Luke 16:19-31

Luke 16

19: There was a certain rich man, which was clothed in purple and fine linen, and fared sumptuously every day:

20: And there was a certain beggar named Lazarus, which was laid at his gate, full of sores,

21: And desiring to be fed with the crumbs which fell from the rich man's table: moreover the dogs came and licked his sores.

22: And it came to pass, that the beggar died, and was carried by the angels into Abraham's bosom: the rich man also died, and was buried;

23: And in hell he lift up his eyes, being in torments, and seeth Abraham afar off, and Lazarus in his bosom.

24: And he cried and said, Father Abraham, have mercy on me, and send Lazarus, that he may dip the tip of his finger in water, and cool my tongue; for I am tormented in this flame.

25: But Abraham said, Son, remember that thou in thy lifetime receivedst thy good things, and likewise Lazarus evil things: but now he is comforted, and thou art tormented.

26: And beside all this, between us and you there is a great gulf fixed: so that they which would pass from hence to you cannot; neither can they pass to us, that would come from thence.

27: Then he said, I pray thee therefore, father, that thou wouldest send him to my father's house:

28: For I have five brethren; that he may testify unto them, lest they also come into this place of torment.

29: Abraham saith unto him, They have Moses and the prophets; let them hear them.

30: And he said, Nay, father Abraham: but if one went unto them from the dead, they will repent.

31: And he said unto him, If they hear not Moses and the prophets, neither will they be persuaded, though one rose from the dead.

Unjust Judge

Luke 18:2-5

Luke 18

2: Saying, There was in a city a judge, which feared not God, neither regarded man:

3: And there was a widow in that city; and she came unto him, saying, Avenge me of mine adversary.

4: And he would not for a while: but afterward he said within himself, Though I fear not God, nor regard man;

5: Yet because this widow troubleth me, I will avenge her, lest by her continual coming she weary me.

Pharisee & Publican

Luke 18:10-14

Luke 18

10: Two men went up into the temple to pray; the one a Pharisee, and the other a publican.

11: The Pharisee stood and prayed thus with himself, God, I thank thee, that I am not as other men are, extortionists, unjust, adulterers, or even as this publican.

12: I fast twice in the week, I give tithes of all that I possess.

13: And the publican, standing afar off, would not lift up so much as his eyes unto heaven, but smote upon his breast, saying, God be merciful to me a sinner.

14: I tell you, this man went down to his house justified rather than the other.

Remembering Chapters & Verses

> *The origin of the phonetic system has been traced back more than 300 years to 1648, when Winckelman (also spelled Wenusheim or Wenssshein) introduced a digit-letter system in which the digits were represented by letters of the alphabet. These letters were then used to represent a given number sequence.*
>
> —Kenneth L. Higbee

> *We are no other than a moving row*
>
> *Of magic shadow-shapes that come and go*
>
> *Round with the sun-illumined Lantern held*
>
> *In Midnight by the Master of the Show*
>
> —Omar Khayyám

Now that you've remembered the names and key details of the parables, you might also want to remember the chapter and verse for each parable. One way to do this is to associate each chapter and verse number with easily remembered images. You can base these images on anything you care to. We suggest a combination of several simple and well-tested methods.

At each parable location in your journey, you'll add images that represent the location of the parable in the New Testament. Specifically, you will use symbolic images to remember the book, chapter, and starting verse of each parable.

Remembering Books: Three Friends

The parables occur in Matthew, Mark, and/or Luke. We suggest you start by trying to remember only one location even if a parable occurs in more than one book. For example, since the book of Mark was likely written first, we list parables that occur in Mark first. Next, we add parables that occurred in Matthew, then parables that occurred in Luke. A few exceptions exist in our order, but these will be clear in the summary table which follows.

To remember that a parable occurs in Matthew, Mark, or Luke, first select three of your friends, family, or people you know who have the names Matthew, Mark, and Luke. If you don't know a person with one of these names, think of someone (movie star, sports star, character in a novel) with the name a variant of these names (*e.g.*,

Matt, Matilda, Markus, Mary, Lukas, Lucy). Whenever you see the person you choose for Matthew, Mark, or Luke, they will remind you of the New Testament book that contains a particular parable.

Next, at the location of the parable (in your country church journey), imagine your friend there. For example, see your friend Mark on the steps with your Sower image. Maybe your friend Mark is the sower. See him scattering seeds. Or maybe Mark is talking to the sower.

Remembering Chapters: 25 Alphabet Images

Parables occur in a chapters between 1 and 25 in Matthew, Mark, and Luke. Therefore, we need to associate 25 images with the numbers 1-25. One of the earliest memory systems associated numbers with each letter of the alphabet. Since you already know your ABCs by heart, this system requires only the additional steps of associating an image for each letter. For example, 1 = A = Apple, 2 = B = Bear, 3 = C = Cat, 4 = D = dog, and so on. Or make up your own number-letter-image associations. If you see an alligator instead of an apple, then designate alligator to represent chapter 1.

To help you recall more quickly which letters are associated with each number, break down the letters of the alphabet into groups of five. As with your landmark locations in your memory journey, make up something special about each five or ten letter image. For example, to remember that Jester = 10, imagine that the jester is performing with a wand and a hoop (which look like a one and a zero). Hear her jingling bells and see her flashy colors. Make her

Alphabet Images

1. Apple
2. Bear
3. Cat
4. Dog
5. ELEPHANT
6. Fish
7. Goose
8. Horse
9. Igloo
10. JESTER
11. Kangaroo
12. Leopard
13. Moose
14. Nacho
15. OCTOPUS
16. Panda
17. Queen
18. Rabbit
19. Skunk
20. TIGHT-ROPE WALKER
21. Umbrella
22. Violin
23. Watermelon
24. Xylophone
25. YARN
26. Zebra

> **Note**
> *Since chapters containing parables only go through 25, learning an alphabet image for 26 is not necessary. Similarly, learning a number shape or rhyme for 10 is not necessary since 10 is remembered with 1 and 0. However, it can be handy to have these symbols for use in other memory tasks.*

stand out. Think about your fives and tens for an extra moment and consider why they're special, so you can easily jump to them. This way, when you come across Violin in your image journey, instead of counting A, B, C, to see what number Violin (or V) represents, you will know that Tight-rope Walker (T) is twenty. So just count: T, U, V—20, 21, 22; Violin = chapter 22.

Once you decide on a set of 25 images to represent chapters 1-25, then every time a parable occurs, for example, in chapter 1 of a particular book, see an apple (with the friend that represents the book) at the location where you store that parable in your memory journey. The Sower parable occurs in Mark, chapter 4. Therefore, when you see the sower talking to your friend Mark, notice that Mark is petting a friendly Dog (Dog = D = 4). To make this image or scene more vivid, add a feature or detail to the Dog. Perhaps it's a black Labrador Retriever who is wagging his tail.

Remembering Verses: Shapes & Rhymes

Remembering verses is trickier because the verses in some chapters where parables occur are quite high. The parable of the Great Fish, for example, occurs in Matthew, chapter 13, beginning with verse 47. Thus, we suggest you create a memory system for remembering numbers 0-9 (or up to 10). To remember two-digit numbers, just combine two images, each representing one single digit. Thus, to remember verse 47, you associate two images: one for 4 and another for 7.

One simple way to remember numbers 0-9 is to associate each number with a shape. What does each number look like? You may also use rhymes for the single digit. What does each number sound like? Consider using number shapes to remember a first digit and rhymes to remember a second digit. So to remember 47 (4-shape = sailboat + 7-rhyme = heaven), you might see a sailboat sailing through the clouds to heaven.

Add these verse image details to your memory journey. For example, for the Sower (Mark 4:3): At the steps, see the Sower (parable) talking to Mark (book), who is petting his Dog (chapter). Why is he petting his dog? His poor dog is Handcuffed—or pawcuffed—(number shape for verse 3).

Thus, when someone asks where the Sower parable is located, you see the scene at the steps. You see your friend Mark there, which reminds you of the Book of Mark. You see his dog, which reminds you of the number four, or chapter four. And the handcuffs remind you of the number three, or verse three. Mark 4:3.

Number Shapes

0. Ball or Pool
1. Candle
2. Swan
3. Handcuffs
4. Sailboat
5. Pregnant Woman
6. Elephant Trunk
7. Boomerang
8. Snowman
9. Balloon on String
10. Bat & Ball

Number Rhymes

0. Cheerio™
1. Gun
2. Shoe
3. Tree
4. Door
5. Hive
6. Sticks
7. Heaven
8. Gate
9. Twine
10. Grin

The Complete System

1. PARABLE: symbolic image at journey location

2. BOOK where the parable first occurred: friend who represents Mark, Matthew, or Luke

3. CHAPTER: alphabet image (1-25)

4. VERSE where the parable begins: number shapes/rhymes

It should be apparent by now that you can add as much information as you want to a location. Each detail you add at a journey location is another piece of information you want to remember about the main item you've put there (*e.g.*, the parable). You are in effect creating a scene at a location that represents the information you want to remember.

This may sound complex, but it's surprisingly easy to do because your memory wants to associate images. That's memory's nature. When you see an image in a place clearly, you remember it surprisingly easily. If you want to continue remembering it, return to your journey from time to time and see the scene images at each location. After a few return trips, you'll discover that you remember the images without even trying.

To make this easier for you, we'll map out the book-chapter-verse locations of the 30 parables in the remainder of this chapter. As always, you need not remember the particular images we've chosen. This example's intention is to show you concretely how it's done. We've learned that abstract descriptions are not memorable, only concrete ones are.

Church Location	Parable Symbol	Book	Chapter:Verse	Alphabet	Shape/Rhyme
Steps	Sower	Mark	4:3	Dog	Handcuffs
Porch	Seed Growing Secretly	Mark	4:26	Dog	Swan-Sticks
Left Post	Wicked Tenants	Mark	12:1	Leopard	Candle
Right Post	Budding Fig Tree	Mark	13:28	Moose	Swan-Gate
DOOR	Leaven	Matthew	13:33	Moose	Handcuffs-Tree
Back Left Pew	Treasure	Matthew	13:44	Moose	Sailboat-Door
Back Left Window	Pearl	Matthew	13:45	Moose	Sailboat-Hive
Middle Left Pew	Great Fish	Matthew	13:47	Moose	Sailboat-Heaven
Front Left Window	Lost Sheep	Matthew	18:12	Rabbit	Candle-Shoe
FRONT LEFT PEW	Unforgiving Servant	Matthew	18:23	Rabbit	Swan-Tree
Altar	Vineyard Workers	Matthew	20:1	Tight-rope Walker	Candle
Pulpit	Two Sons	Matthew	21:28	Umbrella	Swan-Gate
Choir	Lamps & Virgins	Matthew	25:1	Yarn	Candle
Font	Talents	Matthew	25:14	Yarn	Candle-Door
PIANO	Wine Bottles	Luke	5:37	Elephant	Handcuffs-Heaven
Front Right Pew	Good Samaritan	Luke	10:30	Jester	Handcuffs-Cheerio
Front Right Window	Friend at Midnight	Luke	11:5	Kangaroo	Pregnant Woman
Middle Right Pew	Good Gifts	Luke	11:11	Kangaroo	Candle-Gun
Back Right Window	Rich Farmer	Luke	12:16	Leopard	Candle-Sticks
BACK RIGHT PEW	Thief	Luke	12:35	Leopard	Handcuffs-Hive
Steeple	Barren Fig Tree	Luke	13:6	Moose	Elephant Trunk
Roof	Mustard Seed	Luke	13:18	Moose	Candle-Gate
Grass	Great Supper	Luke	14:16	Nacho	Candle-Sticks
Sign	Tower Builder	Luke	14:28	Nacho	Swan-Gate
PARKING	Lost Coin	Luke	15:8	Octopus	Snowman
Parsonage	Prodigal Son	Luke	15:11	Octopus	Candle-Gun
Cemetery Gate	Unjust Steward	Luke	16:1	Penguin	Candle
Marble Gravestone	Rich Man & Lazarus	Luke	16:19	Penguin	Candle-Twine
Wood Cross	Unjust Judge	Luke	18:2	Rabbit	Swan
OAK TREE	Pharisee & Publican	Luke	18:10	Rabbit	Candle-Cheerio

Church Location	Parable Symbol	Book Chapter:Verse	Alphabet	Shape/Rhyme
Steps	Sower	Mark 4:3	Dog	Handcuffs

At the steps, *the* sower *hands* Mark *some seeds.* Mark *is petting his* dog *to cheer him up since the* dog *is* paw-cuffed.

Porch	Seed Growing Secretly	Mark 4:26	Dog	Swan-Sticks

Mark *steps up to the* porch *and kneels to see tiny* seedlings *popping through the floorboards. He feels the boards are smooth like an iced over lake, and he sketches in the imaginary ice a* swan stick-*figure.*

Left Post	Wicked Tenants	Mark 12:1	Leopard	Candle

Mark *steps to the* left side of the porch *and begins dancing with the* wicked tenants*. But then a* leopard *leaps toward them, and Mark springs forward to fend off the leopard with a lit* candle.

Right Post	Budding Fig Tree	Mark 13:28	Moose	Swan-Gate

Exhausted from the tenants and the leopard, Mark *stumbles over to the* right side of the porch *and leans against the* budding fig tree*. He notices a peaceful* moose *munching on a bud. The* swan *Mark drew earlier has come to life, and the swan is forcing its way through a* gate *so it can come eat some fig buds too!* Mark *is tired from his adventure and decides to nap and go no further.*

DOOR	Leaven	Matthew 13:33	Moose	Handcuffs-Tree

Your friend, Matt, *appears with more energy, lured to the* door *by the smell of fresh* bread*. But the* moose *smells it too.* Matt *is not about to let the moose get the bread, so he extracts a pair of* handcuffs *from his back pocket and secures the moose to a* tree.

Back Left Pew	Treasure	Matthew 13:44	Moose	Sailboat-Door

Matt *enters the church and sits reverently at the* back left pew*. Beside him he notices a* treasure *chest. Inside he finds a golden* moose*. Afraid that this might be considered an idol,* Matt *puts the golden moose on a* sailboat *and pushes it toward the* door.

Back Left Window	Pearl	Matthew 13:45	Moose	Sailboat-Hive

Pondering the definition of "idol," Matt *walks to the nearest* window (back left) *and looks out. He sees the same golden* moose *on the* sailboat*, which is sailing toward a bee* hive.

Middle Left Pew	Great Fish	Matthew 13:47	Moose	Sailboat-Heaven

The boat splashes water into the church, and Matt *suddenly has to swim to the* middle (left) pew *as he imagines that he has become a* great fish *swimming around a tropical reef. Gold light flashes above him. He looks up and sees his golden* moose *in that same old* sailboat*, which is now lifting off the water and soaring toward* heaven.

Church Location	Parable Symbol	Book Chapter:Verse	Alphabet	Shape/Rhyme
Front Left Window	Lost Sheep	Matthew 18:12	Rabbit	Candle-Shoe

Sad that his moose has obviously died and gone to heaven, Matt stands and looks out the front left window. He sees a lonely sheep standing in the grass. Just as Matt is wishing the sheep had a friend, a rabbit bounces into view. The rabbit lifts up a candle so the sheep can see enough to tie his shoes and go home.

FRONT LEFT PEW	Unforgiving Servant	Matthew 18:23	Rabbit	Swan-Tree

*Matt is pleased that the sheep is heading home, so he sits at the front (left) pew to thank God, only to be confronted by a **servant** who reprimands Matt for taking the servant's seat in the pew. Matt apologizes, but the servant is **unforgiving**. So Matt slides down the slick pew feeling like an embarrassed swan. He slides and slides until he crashes into a thick tree.*

Altar	Vineyard Workers	Matthew 20:1	Tight-rope Walker	Candle

Feeling repentant, Matt decides to take communion, so he walks up to the altar and asks the vineyard workers for some wine. They say that he must prove himself by walking a tight rope over to the pulpit while holding a candle.

Pulpit	Two Sons	Matthew 21:28	Umbrella	Swan-Gate

Matt arrives safely at the pulpit where is greeted by two sons in a stroller. It's starting to rain on the boys, so Matt holds an umbrella over them. He hands them a stuffed swan toy and pushes them to the gate leading into the choir loft.

Choir	Lamps & Virgins	Matthew 25:1	Yarn	Candle

At the choir loft, Matt sees ten virgins holding unlit lamps. He expects them to stand and sing, but instead they pull out their yarn and start knitting. But it's too dark, so he hands them a candle to light their lamps.

Font	Talents	Matthew 25:14	Yarn	Candle-Door

Since the virgins refuse to sing, Matt strolls over to check out the baptismal font. It looks more like a wishing well because it's full of coins—talents! Disturbed by the desecration, he fills the font/wishing well with yarn and sets it on fire with a candle. The font ablaze breaks through the floor, providing Matt with an escape door.

PIANO	Wine Bottles	Luke 5:37	Elephant	Handcuffs-Heaven

Matt has escaped, and Luke plays honky-tonk piano to celebrate. He takes a swig from the old wine bottle and starts seeing visions: a dancing elephant with hand(foot)cuffs. The elephant is in a circus—it's been a hard life, but Luke knows the elephant will soon be in heaven.

| Church Location | Parable Symbol | Book Chapter:Verse | Alphabet | Shape/Rhyme |

Front Pew — Good Samaritan — Luke 10:30 — Jester — Handcuffs-Cheerio

Luke decides that life is short, so he gets up from the piano and, like the good Samaritan, helps up a crippled man who had been sitting on the front (right) pew. The cripple suddenly begins dancing like a jester, spinning round and round. Luke realizes he's helped a crazy man, so he handcuffs the jester to the pew and gives him a bowl of Cheerios for nourishment.

Front Window — Friend at Midnight — Luke 11:5 — Kangaroo — Pregnant Woman

Luke hears a knock at the front (right) window and looks out to see a friend in the midnight moonlight. The friend is riding like a joey in a kangaroo's pouch. The kangaroo is going slowly because she is also pregnant!

Middle Pew — Good Gifts — Luke 11:11 — Kangaroo — Candle-Gun

Luke sits at the middle (right) pew, which is lined with gifts. He picks one up and gives it to the kangaroo for a baby shower gift. The kangaroo opens the gift and finds a candle. The rambunctious cow-girl kangaroo pretends the candle is a gun, fakes two shots, and gallops off into the sunset.

Back Window — Rich Farmer — Luke 12:16 — Leopard — Candle-Sticks

Luke looks out the back (right) window and sees a farmer building a very tall silo. A leopard leaps onto the top of the silo. Perfectly balanced, the leopard starts banging on the silo like a drum—using candles for drum sticks.

BACK PEW — Thief — Luke 12:35 — Leopard — Handcuffs-Hive

Luke sits back down on the back (right) pew next to a thief, who slips Luke's wallet out of his pocket and bolts for the door. Luke chases her like a leopard and handcuffs her to a bee hive in the back of the church.

Steeple — Barren Fig Tree — Luke 13:6 — Moose — Elephant Trunk

Worried that bees might sting him, Luke climbs up to the steeple. There he perches in the barren fig tree that grows from the steeple, and he sees a moose walking along the roof beam toward him. The moose has a growth coming out of his head that looks like an elephant's trunk.

Roof — Mustard Seed — Luke 13:18 — Moose — Candle-Gate

Frightened, Luke jumps down to the roof, but slips on the mustard seeds that are rolling across the roof. He aborts his fall from the roof by clinging to a candle lodged in a gutter. But the candle breaks, and he slips, landing on a gate below.

Church Location	Parable Symbol	Book	Chapter:Verse	Alphabet	Shape/Rhyme
Grass	Great Supper	Luke	14:16	Nacho	Candle-Sticks

Luke *brushes off and realizes he's standing where the congregation is having a* great picnic supper. *A woman hands him a* nacho, *which revives him, and he begins to feel a Latino rhythm coming on. Someone else hands him a* candle, *which he uses as a drum* stick *to tap a cool beat.*

Sign	Tower Builder	Luke	14:28	Nacho	Swan-Gate

Luke *dances over to the* sign *in front of the church. Someone has constructed a replica of the* Eiffel Tower *beside the sign. Luke downs another* nacho *for energy and scales the tower. From the top, he sees a* swan *flying toward a distant iron* gate.

PARKING	Lost Coin	Luke	15:8	Octopus	Snowman

Luke *effortlessly drops from the tower into the* parking *lot. His foot kicks something—a* coin! *A quarter, probably a child's lost offering. "No!" shouts the* octopus *that approaches Luke, "That's my twenty-five cent piece!" The octopus snatches the coin from Luke, and, using its many long legs, stamps the coin into the face of a* snowman.

Parsonage	Prodigal Son	Luke	15:11	Octopus	Candle-Gun

The enraged octopus *chases Luke to the* parsonage. *Fortunately, the* prodigal son *is waiting to help and fends off the* octopus *with a burning* candle *and a* gun.

Cemetery Gate	Unjust Steward	Luke	16:1	Penguin	Candle

Luke *walks to the* cemetery gate, *which is guarded by an* unjust *snobby* steward. *Luke thinks the steward, dressed in black and white, looks more like a* penguin. *The penguin-steward lights a* candle *and reluctantly guides Luke into the cemetery.*

Marble Gravestone	Rich Man & Lazarus	Luke	16:19	Penguin	Candle-Twine

Luke *stops at the first* marble gravestone *where a* rich man *is lifting* Lazarus *up from the dead. The* penguin *sets his* candle *on the gravestone and ties the two men together with* twine.

Wood Cross	Unjust Judge	Luke	18:2	Rabbit	Swan

Luke *walks to the adjacent* wooden cross. *A* judge *is banging on the cross with his wooden gavel. This noise scares a* rabbit *out of the brush, and a startled* swan *lifts off into the sky.*

OAK TREE	Pharisee & Publican	Luke	18:10	Rabbit	Candle-Cheerio

Luke, *weary from his journey, rests under the* oak tree *and listens to the* Pharisee and publican *while they pray. The* rabbit *realizes that Luke is tired, and she hops over, lights a dinner* candle, *and serves Luke a bowl of* Cheerios.

Mysticism, Meditation, & Sacred Memory

Monastic rhetoric developed an art for composing meditative prayer that conceives of composition in terms of making a "way" among "places" or "seats," or as climbing the steps of a "ladder."

—Mary Carruthers

Therefore whosoever heareth these sayings of mine, and doeth them, I will liken him unto a wise man, which built his house upon a rock.

—Matthew 7:24

A Bible Command

Linking memory to spirituality is at least as old as the Old Testament, where people are frequently admonished to remember God's presence:

> *And thou shalt remember all the way which the LORD thy God led thee these forty years in the wilderness, to humble thee, and to prove thee, to know what was in thine heart.* (Deuteronomy 8:2).

Throughout the Old Testament, people are told to remember (*e.g.*, to "remember these things" in Isaiah 44:21). In the New Testament, the new Christians are told to "remember Jesus Christ" (2 Timothy 2:8). The early desert fathers took scriptural admonitions literally and used them as the basis of their mystical prayer. The name of their technique is sometimes translated as the Practice of the Presence of God. The Greek phrase describing this process, *mneme theou*, means the "Memory of God" (Carruthers 1998).

Know Thyself and Thy God

Today, as in the past, by contemplating (or meditating) on what we've remembered, we remember better and more thoroughly, and we come to know ourselves more fully. According to Thomas Aquinas, we should "meditate often on the things we've memorized since we better recall things that we understand through contemplation."

As western monasticism developed during the Middle Ages, thoughtful reading and memorization of scriptural texts became a key devotional practice. In the monastic tradition, the technical Art of Memory of the classic Roman writers was applied to memorizing scripture. For example, Hugh of St. Victor recommends visualizing Noah's Arc (Carruthers 1998). He places verses of scripture on the steps of a ladder leading up to the arc. The ladder represents one's spiritual progress from the bottom to the top of the arc. The steps of the ladder are locations (a compressed journey) for placing memory images, just as the rooms of your house can be the locations for memory images.

In the monastic tradition, the goal of memorizing became more than just a system for recalling information. It became a system for contemplation, where the memorizer "saw with his heart the truth of hidden things" (Clanchy 1993). Thus, memory was no longer simply the recollection of items on a list, but recollection in the sense of drawing within and remembering God or spiritual matters. By the 13th century, the two meanings had mixed and blended into an Art of Memory that was essentially meditation (Carruthers 1998).

For hundreds of years (from the Middle Ages until the late Renaissance), meditation and meditative reading were widely recommended to the secular clergy and laity. The faithful were encouraged to examine themselves spiritually through meditative exercises. One Art of Memory, for example, used images of the seven Vices and Virtues to recall good deeds and sins (Carruthers and Ziolkowski 2002).

If anyone asks me, however, what is the only and great Art of Memory, I shall say that it is exercise and labor. To learn much by heart, to meditate much and, if possible, daily, are the most efficacious of all methods. Nothing is so much strengthened by practice or weakened by neglect as memory.

—Quintilianus

Marcus Fabius Quintilianus (ca. 35-100) was a Roman rhetorician who wrote about the Art of Memory.

Art and the Art of Memory

The Art of Memory influenced religious thought in the artwork of the 14th century. For example, the illustrations of Psalter of Robert de Lisle include devotional images of the life of Jesus, his crucifixion, and the Madonna. By the 15th century, elaborate image systems were pervasive, for example, in the image of the Wheel of Fortune, which consisted of seven circles, each divided into seven sections. Dante's poem, "The Inferno," can also be regarded as a memory system (Yates 1966).

Imagine a stained glass window. It contains many details and symbolic images. A stained glass window invites contemplation. With light streaming, the colors captivate us. In a time when masses were still given in Latin, people could contemplate God in the cathedral windows even if they could not understand the foreign language being spoken to them. Some stained glass windows in ancient cathedrals indicate complete scenes and histories. These were likely intended to be used as an Art of Memory. Our country church Art of Memory system in this book is based on "cathedral memory systems" of many centuries ago.

The tradition of meditating on mental images reaches a significant spiritual peak with the publication of "The Spiritual Exercises" of St. Ignatius Loyola in 1548. St. Ignatius taught a meditative Art of Memory intended to "bring the soul closer to the spirit." His exercises detail how the meditator should mentally see the images of Jesus or the Virgin Mary in particular locations.

St. Ignatius' First Prelude

The First Prelude is a composition, seeing the place.

Here it is to be noted that, in a visible contemplation or meditation—as, for instance, when one contemplates Christ our Lord, Who is visible—the composition will be to see with the sight of the imagination the corporeal place where the thing is found which I want to contemplate.

I say the corporeal place, as for instance, a Temple or Mountain where Jesus Christ or Our Lady is found, according to what I want to contemplate...

—St. Ignatius Loyola

Holy Cards, Images, & Symbols for Meditation

Inspired by stunning paintings of Jesus and the saints, the first holy cards appeared early in the 15th century. These are similar to early Tarot decks of the period and were likely used for remembering. Originally, holy cards were portable woodcut prints that provided an inexpensive way to have handy inspiring images of patron saints for viewing and meditation. Many of the older holy cards included symbols to associate with the saints. For example, St. Veronica holds the holy napkin with Jesus' face on it. Snakes entwine St. Patrick's feet. John the Baptist baptizes Jesus.

When holy cards are ordered, one has a ready-made journey for the Art of Memory. Each card takes the place of a location on a memory journey. As in a stained glass image or set of images, a holy card can become as complex as you want for your specific memory task. Then, as in any memory journey, you can associate new things you want to remember with the cards and their places.

Ignatius of Loyola (1491-1556) was a knight, hermit, and priest who founded the Society of Jesus (the Jesuits). His exercises are an excellent example of how the monasteries used the Art of Memory to contemplate spiritual matters.

Practice Your Sacred Art

Meditating on your memory journeys and images is a central and on-going part of learning by heart, as is observing, ordering, concentrating, and imagining. By practicing your Art of Memory your remembering becomes a sacred memory art.

Remember—your memory is a treasure and an enduring gift.

Recommended Reading

Art of Memory: Ancient, Medieval, Renaissance, & Pre-Modern Sources

Anonymous. *Dissoi Logoi* Or *Dialexeis* (*ca.* 400 B.C.). Translated by Rosamond Kent Sprague. The Older Sophists. Hackett Publishing Company. 2001.

Anonymous, *Rhetorica Ad Herennium*. Translated by Harry Caplan. Harvard University, Loeb classical Library. 1954.

Aquinas, Thomas. *Summa Theologica*. Translated by Fathers of the English Dominican Province. Benzinger Brothers. 1947.

Aristotle. On the soul. *Parva Naturalia*. On Breath. Leob Classical Library No. 288. Translated by W. S. Hett. 1975.

Bruno, Giordano. "A General Account of Bonding" from Cause, Principle and Unity. Translated by Richard J. Blackwell. Cambridge. 1997.

Bruno, Giordano. *Cantus Circaeus*, The Incantations of Circe; Together with The Judiciary Being the Art of Memory. Translated by Darius Klein. Ouroboros Press. 2009.

Cicero, On the Orator, Books I-II, Translated by E.W. Hutton and H. Rackham. Harvard University, Loeb Classical Library. 1948.

Feinaigle, M. Gregor Von. The New Art of Memory. Sherwood, Neely, and Jones. 1813.

Quintilianus, Marcus Fabius. *Institutio Oratoria*. Translated by H.E. Butler. Loeb Classical Library. Cambridge: Harvard University press, 1920.

St. Ignatius Loyola. Spiritual Exercises of Saint Ignatius, Translated by Anthony Mottola. Doubleday. 1964.

Art of Memory: Modern Resources

Buzan, Tony. Use Your Perfect Memory. Plume/Penguin. 1991.

Carruthers, Mary. The Book of Memory. Cambridge University. 1990.

Carruthers, Mary. The Craft of Thought. Cambridge University. 1998.

Carruthers, Mary and J. M. Ziolkowski (Eds.), The Medieval Craft of Memory. University of Pennsylvania. 2002.

Clanchy, Michael T. From Memory to Written Record: England 1066-1307. Wiley-Blackwell. 2nd Edition. 1993.

Entsminger, Gary L. and S.E. Elliott. Ophelia's Ghost. Pinyon Publishing. 2008.

Higbee, Kenneth L. Your Memory: How it Works & How to Improve It. Marlowe & Company. 1996.

Luria, A. R. The Mind of A Mnemonist. Basic Books. 1968.

O'Brien, Dominic. How to Develop a Brilliant Memory. Duncan Baird. 2005.

Yates, Frances A. The Art of Memory. University of Chicago. 1966.

Modern Studies of Jesus' Parables & Sayings

Crossan, John D. The Birth of Christianity. HarperSanFrancisco. 1998.

Crossan, John D. In Parables. Harper & Row. 1973.

Dodd, C. H. The Parables of the Kingdom. Charles Scribner's Sons. 1961.

Ehrman, B.D. Lost Christianities: The Batttles for Scripture and the Faiths We Never Knew. Oxford U. Press. 2005.

Funk, Robert W., R. W. Hoover, and the Jesus Seminar. The Five Gospels. Polebridge Press. 1993.

Hultgren, Arland J. The Parables of Jesus, a Commentary. Wm. B. Eerdmans Publishing. 2000.

Jeremias, Joachim. Rediscovering the Parables. Charles Scribner's Sons. 1966.

Julicher, Adolf. An Introduction to the New Testament. Translated by Janet Penrose Ward. G.P. Putnam's Sons. 1904.

Kloppenberg, John S. Q. The Earliest Gospel. Westminster John Knox Press. 2008.

Mitchell, Stephen. The Gospel According to Jesus. HarperPerennial. 1991.

Patterson, Stephen J., J. M. Robinson, and H-G Bethge. The Fifth Gospel. Trinity Press International. 1998.

Perrin, Norman. Rediscovering the Teaching of Jesus. Harper & Row. 1967.

Perrin, Norman. Jesus and the Language of the Kingdom. Fortress Press. 1976.

Sanders, E. P. The Historical Figure of Jesus. Allen Lane, The Penguin Press. 1993.

Snodgrass, Kyle R. Stories With Intent: A Comprehensive Guide to the Parables of Jesus. Wm B. Eerdmans Publishing. 2008.

Poetry and Philosophy

FitzGerald, Edward, trans. Rubáiyát of Omar Khayyám. Random House 1947.

Herbert, George. The Complete English Poems. Penguin Classics. 1991.

Kafka, Franz. The Blue Octavo Notebooks. Exact Change. 1991.

Kafka, Franz. Parables. Schocken Books. 1935.

Sewell, Elizabeth. The Orphic Voice. Yale University. 1960.

Spears, Monroe K. The Poetry of W. H. Auden. Oxford University. 1963.

Spurgeon, Caroline. Shakespeare's Imagery and what it tells us. Cambridge University. 1935.

Stevens, Wallace. Collected Poems. Alfred Knopf. 1969.

Stuart, Dabney. Tables. Pinyon Publishing. 2009.

Tolstoy, Leo. The Gospel in Brief. University of Nebraska. 1997.

Traherne, Thomas. Centuries of Meditations. P. J. & A.E. Dobell. 1927.

Wittgenstein, Ludwig. Zettel. Basil Blackwell. 1967.

Yeats, W. B. Collected Poems. Macmillan and Co. 1952.

Index

A
Ad Herennium 26, 42, 154
Aquinas, Thomas 15, 18, 23, 27, 28, 29, 150, 154
Aristotle 25, 154
Ars memoria 26, 27
Art of Memory 14, 15, 17, 23, 25, 26, 27, 28, 29, 30, 36, 40, 151, 152, 153, 154, 155
Auden, W. H. 16

B
Barren Fig Tree 52, 57, 103, 133, 145, 148
Brewer, Ebenezer Cobham 23
Bruno, Giordano 18, 27, 39, 40, 51, 154
Budding Fig Tree 52, 53, 69, 124, 145, 146
Buzan, Tony 155

C
Carruthers, Mary 24, 150, 155
Cicero 15, 17, 26, 27, 28, 154
Clanchy, Michael T 155
Common Sayings 19
Country church 30, 41, 42, 45, 52, 141, 152
Crossan, John Dominic 20
  Crossan 16, 19, 156

D
Dante 152
Dialexeis 15, 27, 36, 51, 154
Dodd, C. H. 50, 156

E
Ehrman, B.D. 156
Entsminger, Gary L 155

F
Feinaigle, M. Gregor Von 27, 30, 154
Figurative language 16, 51
FitzGerald, Edward 157
Friend at Midnight 52, 56, 95, 131, 145, 148
Funk, Robert W. 156

G
Good Gifts 52, 56, 97, 131, 145, 148
Good Samaritan 16, 52, 56, 93, 131, 145, 148
Gospel of Thomas 15, 19, 20, 21
Great Fish 38, 50, 52, 54, 77, 125, 142, 145, 146
Great Supper 52, 57, 107, 133, 145, 149
Greece 14, 17

H
Heart 19, 22, 23, 24, 25, 29, 34, 36, 46, 59, 141, 150, 151, 153
  Heart-mind learning 25
  The HeartMath Solution 25
Herbert, George 13, 157
Higbee, Kenneth L. 140, 155
Holy cards 153
Hultgren, Arland J. 20, 156

I
Image 23, 28, 29, 36, 37, 38, 39, 40, 41, 42, 50, 52, 56, 140, 141, 142, 143, 144, 152, 153
  Alphabet Images 141

J
Jeremias, Joachim 156
  Jeremias 16
Jesus 14, 15, 16, 17, 18, 19, 20, 21, 24, 25, 30, 51, 59, 63, 71, 121, 122, 124, 125, 126, 128, 130, 131, 132, 134, 150, 152, 153, 156
Journey 28, 29, 30, 31, 32, 33, 34, 35, 39, 42, 45, 46, 50, 52, 58, 59, 89, 128, 131, 135, 140, 141, 142, 143, 144, 149, 151, 153
Julicher, Adolf 156

K
Kafka, Franz 17, 32, 157
Khayyám, Omar 140
Kingdom of heaven 16, 51, 65, 81, 83, 105, 107, 124, 125, 126, 127, 128, 133, 134
King James 15, 20, 21, 51
Kloppenberg, John S. Q. 156

L
Lamps & Virgins 52, 55, 87, 128, 145, 147
Landmark location 33
Latin 17, 23, 152
Learn by heart 23
Learn by rote 23
Learning by heart 23, 153
Leaven 52, 53, 71, 124, 145, 146
Lost Coin 52, 57, 111, 135, 145, 149
Lost Sheep 50, 52, 54, 79, 126, 145, 147
Loyola, St. Ignatius 18, 152
  Saint Ignatius 154
Luke 15, 18, 19, 20, 21, 52, 121, 122, 123, 124, 125, 126, 128, 129, 130, 131, 132, 133, 134, 135, 136, 137, 138, 140, 141, 144,

145, 147, 148, 149
Luria, A. R. 155

M

Mark 13, 15, 18, 19, 20, 21, 52, 121, 122, 123, 124, 130, 133, 140, 141, 142, 143, 144, 145, 146
Marsh, Herbert 18
Matthew 15, 16, 18, 20, 21, 36, 52, 122, 123, 124, 125, 126, 127, 128, 130, 131, 133, 134, 140, 141, 142, 144, 145, 146, 147, 150
Memory 14, 15, 17, 23, 24, 25, 26, 27, 28, 29, 30, 35, 36, 37, 40, 42, 45, 46, 141, 142, 143, 144, 151, 152, 153
- Art of Memory. *See* Art of Memory
- Intentional memory 26
- Long-term memory 26
- Memory journey 28, 29, 30, 42, 45, 46, 52, 141, 142, 143, 151, 153
- Memory of God 150
- Short-term memory 26
Middle Ages 18, 27, 151
Mitchell, Stephen 156
Mustard Seed 52, 57, 105, 133, 145, 148

N

New Testament 17, 19, 21, 140, 141, 150, 156
Number Rhymes 143
Number Shapes 143

O

O'Brien, Dominic 15, 27, 28, 38, 155
Old Testament 150
Oral tradition 14, 17, 19

P

Palestine 14, 17
Parable 16, 17, 20, 21, 36, 38, 41, 50, 51, 52, 60, 123, 124, 129, 132, 133, 140, 141, 142, 143, 144
Patterson, Stephen J. 19, 156
Pearl 52, 54, 75, 125, 145, 146
Perrin, Norman 156
  Perrin 16
Pharisee & Publican 52, 58, 121, 145, 149
Prodigal Son 52, 58, 113, 135, 145, 149
Psalm 14, 22
Psalter of Robert de Lisle 152

Q

Q Gospel 19
Quintilianus 151, 154

R

Renaissance 18, 27, 151, 154
Rich Farmer 52, 56, 99, 132, 145, 148
Rich Man & Lazarus 52, 58, 117, 137, 145, 149
Rome 14
Rote. *See* Learn by rote

S

Sanders, E. P. 156
Schofield 20, 21
Seed Growing Secretly 52, 53, 65, 122, 145, 146
Senses 38, 39
Sewell, Elizabeth 34, 157
Snodgrass, Kyle R. 20, 156
Sower 52, 53, 63, 122, 141, 142, 143, 145, 146
Spears, Monroe K. 157
Spurgeon, Caroline 38, 157
Stevens, Wallace 60, 157
Stuart, Dabney 13, 157
Sunday school 22

T

Talents 52, 55, 89, 128, 145, 147
Tarot 153
The Inferno 152
Thief 37, 52, 56, 101, 145, 148
Thomas 15, 18, 19, 20, 21, 23, 27, 28, 29, 121, 122, 123, 124, 125, 126, 130, 132, 133, 134, 150, 154, 157
Tolstoy, Leo 157
Tower Builder 52, 57, 109, 135, 145, 149
Traherne, Thomas 19, 157
Treasure 52, 54, 73, 125, 145, 146
Two Sons 52, 55, 85, 127, 147

U

Unforgiving Servant 52, 54, 81, 126, 145, 147
Unjust Judge 52, 58, 119, 138, 145, 149
Unjust Steward 16, 52, 58, 115, 136, 145, 149

V

Vineyard Workers 16, 52, 55, 83, 127, 145, 147

W

Wheel of Fortune 152
Wicked Tenants 52, 53, 67, 123, 145, 146
Wine Bottles 52, 55, 91, 130, 145, 147
Wittgenstein, Ludwig 157
  Wittgenstein 61

Y

Yates, Frances A 155
  Yates 18, 152
Yeats, W. B. 61, 157

www.ingramcontent.com/pod-product-compliance
Lightning Source LLC
Chambersburg PA
CBHW080517090426
42734CB00015B/3085